Richard Graves

Lucubrations

Essays in Prose and Verse

Richard Graves

Lucubrations
Essays in Prose and Verse

ISBN/EAN: 9783744689410

Printed in Europe, USA, Canada, Australia, Japan

Cover: Foto ©Thomas Meinert / pixelio.de

More available books at **www.hansebooks.com**

LUCUBRATIONS.

LUCUBRATIONS:

CONSISTING OF

ESSAYS, REVERIES, &c.

IN PROSE AND VERSE.

LANGUESCIT

By the late PETER OF PONTEFRACT.

Hæc mihi charta nuces; hæc est mihi charta fritillus.
MART.

For cards and dice, with pen and paper
I thus consume the evening taper.

LONDON:
PRINTED FOR J. DODSLEY, PALL-MALL.

M.DCC.LXXXVI.

TO

GRYFFYD PRICE,

OF

Penleagar, in *Glamorganſhire*, Eſq *.

SIR,

THOUGH, from motives of gratitude, I have prefixed ſo reſpectable a name to this miſcellaneous

* A King's Counſel.

 pub-

publication; yet, as I have done it *without* your *permiſſion*, you are certainly not reſponſible for its many defects or its trivial contents.

Our late friend, Poor Peter of Pontefract * (as he generally called himſelf) was thoroughly ſenſible of the idle manner in which he had for ſome years amuſed his leiſure hours; and

* Not the prophet of that name, mentioned in Shakeſpear's King John.—He only alluded to the place whence the family originally came. See Columella, vol. ii. p. 20.

uſed

ufed to apply to himfelf, what Young fays of Dr. Trapp,

"*I am now a* fcribbler, *who was once*
"*a* man."

A fhort explanation of which humiliating confeffion, will be the beft apology to you, Sir, and to fome others of his moft valued friends, for his having thus proftituted that dignity of character, to which they thought he might have afpired: tho' he himfelf was convinced, nature never intended him for higher acquirements. And, when the late B. of G. once ſaid to him, Peter, 'An 'me ſuperbiam,' "Take more upon "you," he anſwered, Your lordſhip might as well bid me add, "two "cubits to my ſtature."

OUR friend Peter, then (as you probably know, Sir) had taken his degrees in the Univerſity with ſome eclat; and was reputed at leaſt a good claſſical ſcholar; ſomewhat of an antiquary; a tolerable adept in the ſciences, and particularly in the ſci-

ence

ence of Divinity, which he intended to make his profeſſion.

But having prematurely (and perhaps a little indiſcreetly) engaged in a matrimonial connexion, and in conſequence involved himſelf, early in life, in domeſtic cares, with only a younger brother's fortune, and very ſlender preferment; he was under a neceſſity of educating his own children; and, in order to make ſome tolerable proviſion for them, to undertake the education of other people's children.

The

The bodily fatigues, and, to an ingenuous *mind*, the more mortifying circumſtances, incident to ſuch an employment; from, ſometimes the juſt, though more frequently the capricious and abſurd expectations of fond parents, rendered him incapable of perſevering in that courſe of ſtudy, which in his youth he had ſketched out, and for ſome time regularly purſued.

" *Ex illo fluere & retrò ſublapſa referri*
" *Spes Danaum*; fractæ vires—."

VIRG.

From

From that time he could only amuſe himſelf, in an evening, with ſuch kind of reading and writing as, in an indolent poſture, lolling in an eaſy chair, or leaning on one elbow, a man may be ſuppoſed to have attended to.

This, Sir, is the true origin of thoſe many flimſy productions of our late friend; which, though they may have diſappointed the expectations of his more judicious acquaintance, have acquired him ſome degree of reputation amongſt thoſe who read with no other view, than that which the author wrote—to amuſe themſelves, and to forget for a time the cares and vexations of human life: of which taſte, however, as he never wrote any thing, he truſts, contrary to the religion of his country or to good manners, our friend thought it allowable ſo far to avail himſelf, as, for theſe ten years paſt, to have indulged himſelf in an annual viſit to the metropolis, without detriment to his family.

"THERE was a time indeed (as Lord Shafteſbury obſerves) when the name

name of Author ſtood for ſomething conſiderable in the world;" but the times are altered. Voltaire mentions a French writer, who begat a child, and wrote a book, every year. Now, though our friend did not pretend to the former manly exploits, yet he, or any young ſpinſter in the kingdom, could perform the latter, and write a book in leſs than nine months.

The Editor, therefore, hopes to ſhelter himſelf from cenſure under the faſhion of the times, in giving to the public theſe Lucubrations, which,

it appears, that, after ſome little
rection, the author himſelf inte
for the preſs.

I am,

SIR,

with the greateſt eſteem,

and ſincereſt attachment,

your obliged,

and affectionate,

humble ſervant,

The EDIT

ERRATA vel MUTANDA.

Page 4. l. 8. read, *which* become.
18. l. 2. r. Hector *and* Andromache; and the like.
19. l. 6. for *should* r. *may*.
24. l. ult. r. *semireducta*.
27. l. 8. dele the mark of reference.
40. l. penult. " with" in italics.
51. l. 12 and 13. dele *their devotees*.
53. l. 10. r. a *very* wife.
69. l. 6. r. *revivification*.
92. l. 1. for *fellow subjects*, r. *brethren*.
115. l. penult. r. *yourselves*.
120. l. penult. r. *amusements*.
128. l. 7. r. *of* them.
138. l. 5. for *Matius* r. *Martius*.
142. additional note to line 10,—' Anch' Io son Pit- ' tore.'
158. l. ult. for *but* r. *her*.
161. l. ult. " to think on me," in italics.
175. note to l. 11.—" Master M—gue."
178. l. 3. r. To Sir Z— S—ple, Bart.
192. l. 11. for *But* r. *When*.

LUCUBRATIONS, &c.

ON

THE POWER OF HABIT.

A PREFATORY ESSAY.

—— tenet insanabile multos
Scribendi cacoëthes.—— JUV.

THE influence of *Habit* on the actions of men, cannot have escaped the notice of the most inattentive observer: and its *general* tendency to produce either a virtuous or vicious conduct, has been so frequently the subject of moral writers, that nothing very new can be ſaid upon the occaſion.

The effects of Habit, both on the bodies and minds of men, are indeed as mechanical, as on thoſe animals which are governed by mere inſtinct.—A ſober citizen goes with the ſame invariable regularity, and with as much ſatisfaction, to his uſual ſeat in the coffee-room, as a pack-horſe to the inn where he has been uſed to feed; and is miſerable if any buſineſs intervenes to deprive him of his evening recreation.

A lady, long accuſtomed to cards, ſits down with as keen an appetite to the whiſt-table in an evening, as an epicure to a haunch of veniſon: and I was not ſurpriſed, that an old dowager, ſome time ſince, at Bath, ſhould expire with the cards in her hand.

Inſtances are unneceſſary on ſo trite a ſubject; yet, I cannot forbear mentioning one

one more, which ſhews, that by *indulging* themſelves in idle habits, men may loſe all reliſh for the beauties of nature, and every amuſement, but that to which they have been long accuſtomed.

I ſome years ſince accompanied an old bachelor, of a genteel profeſſion, in the Strand, to a gentleman's ſeat in St——d-ſhire, with whoſe family he had ſome connexion. After coffee, in the evening, we took a walk together on the lawn; when the declining ſun had ting'd with its golden beams the neighbouring hills, and gave a rich luſtre to every object;— "Well," ſaid I, "this place is quite an "elyſium, and the family are extremely "agreeable; we ſhall ſpend a week here "quite to our ſatisfaction."

"I don't know that," replied my friend;—"the place and the people are "well enough; but I ſhall be glad when we "get back to our club at *The Five Bells.*"

Thus do people, who are habitually attached to any one mode of life, loſe all taſte for every other enjoyment.

There are many amuſements, innocent enough in themſelves, become really criminal when indulged, as they too frequently are by ſolitary people, to a culpable exceſs: ſo that what was at firſt an indifferent, or perhaps a diſagreeable action, becomes at length an inveterate Habit; or, rather, an incurable diſeaſe. Of this kind, are ſmoking tobacco, taking ſnuff, and *ſcribbling*—whether in proſe or verſe. Of theſe, the two former are moſt injurious to the health of thoſe that practiſe them; but the latter proves frequently more pernicious to ſociety, as it is too often employed in corrupting or unſettling the principles of pious chriſtians or peaceful citizens; in disturbing the tranquillity of families, or injuring the characters of individuals.

And when once a man, whether from pique or disappointment, or any other cause, has been engaged on any subject, especially of the polemic kind, for some time, he continues it from Habit, even when the cause is removed, or on very dissimilar occasions. Thus Cato (as every school-boy knows) having once entered the lists, in the debate about the total destruction of Carthage, for ever after, whatever the subject of his speech was, concluded it with—*Delenda est Carthago*—"Carthage must be "demolished." And every patriotic paragraph-writer, though his subject may be the Queen's Birth-day, or the Lord Mayor's shew—ends with complaints of the infringement of our *liberty*, or invading the rights of the subject :—nay, a *disappointed* ecclesiastic, whether churchman or dissenter, even in a *charity* sermon, will growl at the *establishment*, and give a snap at the Trinity.

To this inveterate Habit I would willingly attribute many of the later works of Lord Bolingbroke and Voltaire, against religion and the moral attributes of the Deity: as one cannot conceive any person to be actuated by so diabolical a motive, as, at the age of seventy or eighty, intentionally to strike at the foundation of all morality, and of course at the very existence of society, and the general happiness of mankind.

The later rhymes of Swift, upon every the most trifling occurrence, must, I am persuaded, have been almost the involuntary effects of the same *habitual* indulgence.—But I have often considered with astonishment the fifteen books of Martial's *Epigrams*, as

they

they are called; though the two last consist of 300 insipid distichs, on almost every article of food, or domestic utensils; such as were sent as presents, from one friend to another, at the Saturnalian feasts. The first, I think, is upon

PEPPER.

" *If on your plate a beccafico's plac'd,*
" *Add pepper to it—if you'd shew your taste.*"

He ends with what he should have begun,

BREAKFAST.

" *The cock proclaims the dawn; good folks,*
" *arise!*
" *Hot rolls for breakfast, hark! the baker*
" *cries.*"

The best part of the three hundred are, in point of wit, upon a level with the following *extempore* imitations:

THE TURNIP.

The sweetest turnips grow in open fields,
And, eat with mutton, wholesome diet yields.

THE CABBAGE.

The cabbage in each cottage garden grows;
Its use and flavour every taylor knows.

Which remind us of Swift's ridicule on the bombast of modern tragedy:

" *Snuff the candle.*
" *Yon luminary amputation needs;*
" *So shall ye save its half-extinguish'd*
" *light* *."

The

* The learned editor, and ingenious printer, Henry Stephen, has varied one Greek distich 105 times; most of which, as a proof of this habitual propensity

The author of the following ebullitions of an idle fancy, would willingly ſhelter himſelf under theſe reſpectable examples. And, as "cuſtom has been conſidered as a ſecond "nature," would hope, that his having unfortunately contracted a *Habit* of *ſcribbling*, might be deemed as good a plea, as that of a gentleman, who being reproved for ſwearing, replied, "That he was *born* ſo:"— For, though few people are born either of a *rhyming* or of a *ſwearing* conſtitution, yet the author had actually got a trick of rhyming before he had learned his catechiſm.

propenſity to verſifying, he tells us, were compoſed on horſeback——

ANCHISES to VENUS.

"O Venus (for thou canſt) my youth reſtore,
"Or, now I'm old, ſtill love me, as before."

But, though it should be admitted as some alleviation of a man's folly, who by indulgence has contracted an habitual thirst, that it is become *morally* impossible for him to abstain from drinking—is that any excuse, you will say, for his appearing in *public* in a state of intoxication?—'Ah! there's the 'rub.'——The apology for one's amusing one's self in *private*, runs on fluently enough; but—'Why then publish?'

Pope himself, after many plausible reasons for a poor d—ned poet's perseverance in scribbling, has no other resource, than the partial judgment of friends:

"*Congreve approv'd, and Swift* endur'd
"*my lays.*"

The author of the following Lucubrations, however, has not even this to plead; having, by his solitary situation, been precluded from consulting his few surviving friends, if he had been inclined to involve their credit in the event of such a publication: and some of these pieces, being on temporary subjects, he has ventured into public, to take their chance, with all due submission to the candour of his readers *.

For an Author to say, that he publishes nothing *immoral*, is like Horace's slave, who plumed himself that he had stole nothing; and may expect a similar answer: "Well, "then, you shall not be hanged in chains." But, "can you, Sir, *instruct* the world?"— I might have done so, if I had lived when

* Valerius Maximus has perhaps hinted the true motive for most publications of this trivial kind, in speaking of Fabius Pictor's putting his name to his rude sketches——"Sordido studio deditum ingenium, "qualemcunque illum laborem suum silentio obli-"terari noluit."——B. viii. C. 14.

the world was in its *infancy*. But the world is now older and wiser than I am.—" Can " you then *entertain* the world?"—The world, Sir, can *entertain* itself, with gambling, horse-races, and bruising-matches.

" What then are your pretensions—only " to *amuse* those idle people who will listen " to any thing that is new?"—Why, Sir, I have written to *amuse* myself; and, if the world can amuse themselves with what I have written, they will read my book—if not, waste paper is useful on various occasions: and the printing my book has *employed* several poor d—ls: and the consumption of paper augments the revenue: so that, supposing the national debt (which is now *going* to be paid off) to be 240 millions, nineteen shillings, and eleven pence three farthings, if my works contribute but the odd farthing towards that salutary work,

I have

I have a claim to the minister's acknowledgment and the thanks of the nation.

Some of the following pieces, however, he flatters himself, have at least the merit of a moral *tendency*: and, throughout the whole, the author has been so far from *intending* to make any one unhappy, or less pleased with himself, that he may perhaps be censured for too general a strain of compliment and panegyric.

The reader, however, is not to consider the poetical part of this miscellaneous collection, as always expressive of the author's serious opinion, or real state of his mind (for who will swear to the truth of a song?) but, frequently, as the mere effect of the above-mentioned *cacoethes*, or inveterate habit of scribbling and rhyming, on almost every possible occurrence of human life—on real or imaginary occasions. Accordingly,

he

he writes amorous verses without being in love; and elegies without being greatly concerned. He celebrates beauties whom he never saw, and satyrizes coxcombs with whom he is in perfect charity; for he feels himself possessed of so great a share of philanthropy, or universal love of mankind (and of womankind too) that the good, the bad, and the indifferent, are almost equally objects of his *affection*, though not of his *esteem*.

" *Nihil humani a me alienum puto.*"

I cannot be indifferent to any thing that concerns the good of mankind. I accordingly enjoy every act of benevolence or charity; every prosperous event that befals my country or my friends; and even the sight of every beautiful nymph, that exhibits her charms in the public walks. On these interesting

teresting occasions, my imagination is as mechanically set to work, as a windmill by a brisk gale of wind; and, by celebrating a benevolent action, I seem to share the pleasure with the person that performs it; I gratify, at least, that irresistible propensity to scribbling, which is the effect of that invincible Habit above described.

To caution young people against this habit of *rhyming*, however, is the particular use I would make of these trite reflections.—They may consider it as a kind of dying speech of an old offender; who would exhort them to beware of rhyming company and handsome women, and never to profane the sabbath by reading any other poetry on that day than Sternhold and Hopkins—or such pious strains as have no tendency to elevate and inflame the imagination.—Let them, if they find themselves inclined to it,

try

try their hand at a ſonnet or a ſtanza on their firſt love; but by no means indulge that inclination, unleſs they are conſcious of a truly poetical genius; in which they are very likely to be deceived. Young people, however, of this turn, are like adventurers in a lottery—every one fancies himſelf a favourite of the Muſes: and, though the world rarely beſtows more than one or two laurel crowns in an age, he flatters himſelf that his is the fortunate ticket.

ON

PORTRAIT-PAINTING.

THE learned and ingenious * author of Fitzosborne's Letters has exposed, with considerable humour, and much good sense, the ridiculous vanity of people who, though they have done nothing to merit the notice of the present age, are yet ambitious of exhibiting their persons on canvass, for the satisfaction of posterity. He has also proposed a more ingenious and rational method of having family pictures represented, under some interesting historical subjects, suitable to their rank and character. As an officer, for instance, taking leave of his

* The amiable W. Melmoth, esq.

lady

lady and child, in the characters of Hector, Andromache, and the like.

I cannot but think, however, that this elegant writer has urged his point with too much ſeverity, in the former inſtance; and, in the latter, though he foreſaw ſome enormous abſurdities, which would be the probable conſequence of ſuch a practice being generally adopted, yet methinks he has not ſufficiently expatiated upon that head.

As to the firſt particular then, the author grants, that ſingle portraits are a very proper manner of perpetuating the reſemblance of ſuch individuals as have diſtinguiſhed themſelves either by their actions or by their writings, in their reſpective generations; and, that a deſire of being acquainted with the perſons of ſuch great men, is a natural and reaſonable curioſity.

But ſurely the number of thoſe extraordinary

dinary geniuſes is ſo ſmall, in any given period of time, that it would be difficult to find an artiſt who ſhould think it worth while to qualify himſelf ſufficiently, in that particular branch of painting, to be able faithfully to repreſent thoſe *few*, who ſhould have deſerved that diſtinction. So that if this taſte, ridiculous as it is, had been leſs prevalent in the world, the curioſity of the preſent age, for inſtance, would have loſt the ſatisfaction of viewing the features of Newton or Locke, Milton, Addiſon, or Pope, and many other eminent characters of the laſt or preſent century.

Beſides, if none but perſons of diſtinguiſhed talents were to be honoured with their portraits, where muſt we draw the line? or who ſhall eſtimate the preciſe degree of merit of ſuch individuals, whoſe figures are worthy to be tranſmitted to poſterity? Not only people of different parties, but of different literary purſuits, or of different taſtes, would have their patriots, their heroes, their orators, their poets, their painters, and their fidlers,—and even their preachers, whoſe illuſtrious phyſiognomies they would earneſtly contend to have conſecrated to immortality; each party appealing from the deciſions, and mutually ridiculing the abſurd partialities of each other: ſo that matters would probably ſoon return into their ancient channel; and, in ſpite of the ſneers of the faſtidious connoiſſeur, portrait-painting would regain its popularity, and again become the moſt lucrative branch of the profeſſion.

As to the many abſurdities which would be the natural conſequence of Sir Thomas Fitzoſborne's ingenious ſyſtem, of repreſenting common families under ſome celebrated

hiſtorical

historical subjects, or modern characters under those of the heroic ages; they are indeed so obvious, that the author probably thought them unnecessary to be particularly pointed out, or minutely insisted on.

The complaisance or interested views of some painters, the indolence or limited capacity of others, co-operating with the vanity or ambition of the families that sate to them, would unavoidably produce the most extravagant incongruities.

I remember an itinerant performer, of the lowest rank in his profession (having indeed been only a broken house-painter) who, in a remote province, went about the little market-towns and villages to paint signs. By much practice, he had learned to express, with great facility, a Rose and Crown, a Red Lion, and a Black Bear; so that, whatever subject his customers proposed, he assigned

many

many unanſwerable arguments for their giving the preference to one of the three in which he excelled.

If the landlord deſired the Flower-de-luce, he aſſured him that the Roſe and Crown, as an Engliſh device, would be more lucky, and more attractive of cuſtomers, than what mine hoſt had pitched upon; if another named the White Swan, he recommended the Black Bear; if a third was ambitious of exhibiting the King's Head, he applauded his loyalty, but ſaid, that in this *patriotic* age he ran the riſk of loſing one half of his cuſtomers; and therefore exhorted him, by all means, to make choice of the *Red Lion*.

Something ſimilar to this, would undoubtedly be the conduct of thoſe hiſtorical portrait-painters, whom Fitzoſborne's project is calculated to encourage; which would certainly produce many tragi-comical deſigns,

ſigns, more ludicrous than the family of Dr. Primroſe, in the Vicar of Wakefield; whoſe wife choſe to be drawn in the character of Venus—one daughter as a Shepherdeſs, and the other as an Amazon, in a green joſeph, a cock'd hat, and a whip in her hand.

A wealthy apothecary would naturally wiſh to be repreſented as perſonating a phyſician. Accordingly, the artiſt goes to work, and exhibits the doctor; not in his ſnuff-coloured coat and grizzled wig, but in the Greek *pallium* and philoſophic beard, feeling the pulſe of his booby ſon, in the perſon of Antiochus; whilſt the old lady is complimented as a fit repreſentative of the beautiful Stratonice *.

A fiſhmonger and his wife might well enough be painted (or rather *drawn*) in a

* See Plutarch in Demetrius Poliorcetes.

chaiſe-

chaiſe-marine, under the forms of Neptune and Amphitrite—or, mine hoſt of the ——— tavern, ſitting, like Jupiter, on a cloud inſtead of a cuſhion; and his young wife, like Hebe, preſenting him with wine in a golden goblet: and the limner would doubtleſs explain to them the great propriety of ſuch a repreſentation; yet a ſtranger would find it difficult to reſtrain his riſible muſcles, even in the preſence of the good lady of the houſe, when ſhewn ſo groteſque a family-piece.

A ſkilful artiſt would naturally repreſent Lady —— in the character of the Medicæan Venus, like the ſenſitive plant, * *ſhrinking from the touch*;—yet her ladyſhip would think it as abſurd to be embarraſſed even with the ſlight drapery of the chaſte Diana, —as for the pretty Mrs. ———, who is

* Semireductus. OVID.

laſhing

laſhing her ſix ponies all day, and gambling all night, to be painted like the ſhepherdeſs of the Alps, tending her flocks, or repoſing herſelf under an oak, near a fountain.

We ſhould ſee a Pawnbroker, perhaps, giving audience to his wife, his ſiſter, and his grandmother, in the tent of Darius—or a Brandy-merchant, like the youthful Alexander, taming his hired Bucephalus.—But enormities of this kind would be endleſs.

Not to mention the ſtratagems which young coxcombs of faſhion would be tempted to employ, by tampering with the artiſt, to throw into ſhade, in the back ground, their awkward or unfaſhionable parents—or, even to cover with a veil their venerable mother, or old ſquare-toes, like Agamemnon, in the famous picture of Iphigenia at Aulis; or, perhaps, as was once practiſed on a noble peer, in a hunting-piece, who, enquiring where his own picture was, the painter told him (as he had been inſtructed by the family) that his lordſhip was concealed behind a tree.

In ſhort, though I admire the ingenuity of the author of this propoſed method of repreſenting family pictures, yet I would by no means wiſh to ſee it become a general practice. But, that there may never be wanting a ſet of artiſts, capable of doing juſtice to diſtinguiſhed merit, let not the meaneſt mechanic, or the moſt inſignificant individual, that can *afford* it, be diſcouraged from committing to canvaſs his ſyſtem of features, whatever they be, for the ſatisfaction of his deſcendants. If he can leave his children either fortune, or fame, they will value his portrait. If he cannot do the one, he is at liberty to omit the other.

Let the phyſician, at leaſt, though not a

Sydenham; the lawyer, though not a Black-ſtone; and the divine, though ſomewhat inferior to Sherlock, be ſtill exhibited with the attributes of their reſpective profeſſions: the phyſician with his dreſſed bob; the lawyer with his tie-wig; and the divine with his eaſy chair, turning over Ἡ καινὴ διαθήκη *, to all eternity †. Nor let us, with too much refinement, condemn a practice, which has produced a Reynolds, a Hoare, and a Gainſborough; with many more, little inferior to thoſe excellent artiſts:—but, as *we* have the pleaſure of contemplating the features of Clarendon, Sydney, Locke, and Newton; Milton, Addiſon, Pope, and Swift; together with all the celebrated

* The New Teſtament, in folio.

† Alludes to the picture of a young divine, the ſon of a ſhop-keeper in a Borough town, which covered one ſide of their little parlour, behind the ſhop.

beauties of the laſt age, let the curioſity of future times be gratified with the ſight of our lord Mansfield, lord Camden, and lord Thurlow; our Lowth, our Hurd, and Samuel Johnſon; our amiable Queen, Mrs. M—t—gue, our dutcheſſes of D——e and R———, and a galaxy of blooming beauties; not diſguiſed in Grecian or Roman habits, but as we now love and admire them, —in the ſimple and * elegant taſte which diſtinguiſhes the age we live in—1782.

* N. B. The butter-woman's great coat had not then been ſo generally adopted.

ON

ON

OUR RECEPTION IN PUBLIC PLACES.

"Friendly at Hackney—faithleſs at Whitehall."
POPE.

THERE is an evil under the ſun, which eſcaped the notice even of Solomon's wiſdom and penetration: it is not probable, however, that a prince, born to ſovereign power, ſhould ever have experienced the evil to which I allude; I mean that *cool reception*, or thoſe ſlights, which we often meet with in public, from perſons with whom in private perhaps we have converſed with the utmoſt freedom and familiarity.

This kind of treatment we are moſt likely to meet with from people not diſtinguiſhed themſelves by their rank or fortune, or any extraordinary merit of any kind; who, as the world is too much influenced by appearances, are afraid they will judge leſs favourably of their own conſequence, by obſerving them to be connected with perſons of ordinary appearance, whatever their real, intrinſic merit may be. Perſons of eſtabliſhed characters and known abilities are generally free from theſe apprehenſions, and often take a pleaſure in countenancing a worthy man in public, with whoſe private good qualities they are ſufficiently acquainted.

There is certainly, however, a diſtinction to be made, with regard to certain characters, between the attention which we ought to expect from them in theſe different ſituations.—

tions.—If a man of rank, or in ſome elevated ſituation (in conſequence perhaps of our juvenile acquaintance) receives me at his own houſe, or in a private company, with a good-natured condeſcenſion; that is no reaſon for my expecting the ſame freedom of behaviour in a place of public reſort, or when engaged in the diſcharge of ſome important official employment. A better man than Falſtaff, would deſervedly have met with the ſame repulſe, if he had ſo familiarly thruſt himſelf into the notice of his late companion, prince Hal, in his coronation proceſſion.—And if I had drank a bottle with a chief juſtice, or a lord chancellor, at his own table, I ſhould deſerve to be taken into cuſtody, as prince Hal himſelf was, if I were to nod at or wink upon either as an acquaintance, when ſitting in the King's-bench or the court of Chancery.—

A proper deference to a ſuperior in public, is the greateſt compliment which we can pay him.

A modeſt man, indeed, eſpecially if conſcious of any thing mean in his perſonal appearance (though it would be hard to be entirely baniſhed from the chearful haunts of men, as a ſpectator); yet ſuch a one would naturally wiſh to ſhrink into and be loſt in the crowd, rather than officiouſly thruſt himſelf into the notice of people of diſtinguiſhed rank, though they ſhould happen to be of his acquaintance.

But when a man of our own level (for a liberal education puts every untitled gentleman upon the ſame level) when ſuch a one converſes with you as a friend, or even a common acquaintance; eats, drinks, and laughs with you at a tavern, or in a private family;

and, when you meet in public, affects to be near-ſighted, *peeps* at you through a glaſs, or bows in ſo cool a manner, as to leave ſtrangers to think you impertinent in claiming his acquaintance; ſuch an inſult deſerves not only to be reſented, but puniſhed on the ſpot, by that compendious proceſs—a twiſt of the noſe, or a kick on the br—ch.

Lord B——, indeed, was miſtaken in the etiquette, when he ſtruck off Lord ———'s hat, for not returning his ſalute when walking with a prince of the blood—otherwiſe, the ſpirit with which he acted, deſerves the higheſt applauſe.

If a man has been guilty of any notorious act of villainy, or even breach of honour; he is deſervedly treated with contempt wherever he appears; and it is injurious to morality, and the intereſts of ſociety, that ſuch a one ſhould meet with a more candid treatment.

A man of a liberal profeſſion, after having in a moſt ſcandalous manner violated a moſt ſacred truſt, relative to a public charity—for which he was forced to quit his place of reſidence, and ought for ever to have ſecluded himſelf from ſociety—had the effrontery, in a public place, to accoſt an old acquaintance with his uſual familiarity; who ſaid, with great propriety (though with more ſpirit than, I own, I could have aſſumed) "Sir, I once thought I knew you; but I "was miſtaken:—and I now know you too "well, to acknowledge you as an acquain-"tance."

There was not the ſame reaſon, I truſt, for the ſlight which I ſome time ſince experienced.

An old college acquaintance took a walk, one fine ſummer's morning, and dined with me at my little villa, near the metropolis.

As

As we had not ſeen each other for ſome years, I was happy to find he intended to dine with me. We drank a bottle together; but, in the midſt of our cordial tête-à-tête, a thunder-ſtorm came on, and ſeemed likely to continue the whole evening.—"Peter," ſays my friend, "you ſhall ſend me home "in your poſt-chaiſe."—As he was rather my ſuperior in fortune, I was glad he made ſo free with me—and the chaiſe was immediately at the door. My poſtilion, on his return, got drunk and broke a ſide-glaſs—I comforted myſelf, however, with the thought of having obliged a reſpectable friend, and indiſſolubly cemented what I conſidered as a creditable connection.

The next day, going through the Mall, I met my dear friend; who had tacked himſelf to a party of four or five young fellows, whom a Knight of the Bath, by the influence of his ſtar, had attracted round him.

From a motive of delicacy, I paſſed by them as quick as I could, leſt he ſhould think it neceſſary to acknowledge the trifling favour, which I had the preceding day conferred on him: but, ſo far from it, he returned my ſalute with that ſtately inclination of the head, with which he would have returned the bow of a ſhoe-maker, whom he had juſt paid for a pair of boots.—I could only expreſs my contempt of the ſlight, by turning round and ſpitting acroſs the Mall, in the direction in which he and his party were walking.

Even the clergy, ſuch, I mean, as with a ſmall degree of merit, by a concurrence of accidental circumſtances, have riſen to dignity or great preferment, are too apt to be guilty of this haughtineſs towards their leſs fortunate brethren; particularly, if they have

had

had the *misfortune* to marry an unportioned virgin, allied in the remoteſt degree to a noble family: they muſt never diſgrace their wiſe's relations by taking notice of, much leſs by converſing with (if he ſhould deſire it) his former acquaintance: whence he is expoſed to the ridicule of his equals, and perhaps held in ſecret contempt by his ſuperiors.

Thoſe dignitaries, indeed, who are inveſted with any eccleſiaſtical authority, ought to preſerve a decent kind of ſtate with regard to the inferior clergy within the ſphere of their juriſdiction; yet there is a degree of affability, with which every gentleman knows how to ſoften that ſenſe of ſuperiority, which cannot but be irkſome to a perſon of an ingenuous mind and liberal education. The few prelates of our church, with whom I have the honour to be acquainted, are eminently possessed of this happy talent of relaxing, in some measure, their authority, without violating their dignity. Of this dignity, heightened by politeness, the two Primates of this, and the Lord Primate of our sister kingdom, exhibit a most amiable example.

An high-priest, of a very different character, whom I remembered a servitor in the University, when I was a fellow of a very respectable college; and who a few years since passed by me with the most supercilious reserve, when I would have condescended to take him by the hand (for a condescension I thought it) gave rise to this essay.

A man of a more irritable temper would have vented his spleen on the person of such a fellow—Plexippus would have vented it on his family and extraction—my method was more peaceable, and, I trust, more innocent;

nocent; who, as I trudged home in great dudgeon, only vented my wrath in the following ſtanzas. Though, I confeſs, that, under the firſt ſenſe of the inſult, I was tempted to parody Hamlet's malediction of the prieſt who refuſed Ophelia Chriſtian burial—

" —— *I tell thee*, haughty *prieſt*,
" *A miniſtring angel ſhall thy* curate *be*,
" *When thou art howling*."

But I ſtarted with horror at ſuch a ſuggeſtion: and have ſince lived to ſee this poor creature an object of compaſſion—crippled by the gout, in conſequence of high living; and, at length, mixed with that clay from which we all originally ſprung—and where pride, precedence, and diſtinction, will ceaſe to torment us.

To

To a HAUGHTY DIVINE.

WHILE thus, with lofty airs, you try
To keep us at a diſtance;
We gladly with the terms comply,
Who want not your aſſiſtance.

But when in ſilence we retire,
We bow and ſcrape, 'tis true;
Not that your grandeur we admire—
We ſee you through and through.

Reſerve, you think, procures reſpect;
It may—but bought too dear;
We all reſent your proud neglect,
We *hate* you, but not fear.

That ſtately mien, that dull grimace,
We ſcorn, you may believe:
When with you, wear a ſerious face,
While laughing in our ſleeve.

Your

Your wealth may dazzle vulgar eyes,
(Which ſeems your favourite plan)
But not impoſe upon the wiſe,
Who only view the *man*.

The world is long ſince too diſcerning,
Such artifice is vain;
Amongſt all men of ſenſe and learning,
Equality muſt reign.

ON

THE FEMALE CHARACTER.

THE two ſexes were evidently formed, not merely for continuing the ſpecies, but for the mutual ſolace and aſſiſtance of each other in the duties and toils of life. They have accordingly been endowed by nature with different talents, and diſtinguiſhed by different proportions of the body, and by different qualities of the mind.

" *For contemplation He, and valour form'd;*
" *For ſoftneſs She, and ſweet attractive grace.*"

Strength,

Strength, activity, firmneſs of body, and ourage and conſtancy of mind, are the characteriſtics of the male; ſoftneſs, gentleneſs, and delicacy, are the ornaments of the female ſex.

This diſtinction of character ought to be religiouſly preſerved; and cannot be violated with impunity by either. The man, by ſoftneſs and effeminacy, loſes that authority over the other ſex, which was intended by nature; and the woman, by robuſt and maſculine airs, loſes her power of pleaſing, and forfeits the rights and privileges of her ſex. The truth of theſe maxims every one muſt have experienced.

I had long entertained a tender regard for an amiable, middle-aged woman, in the mercantile line of life; but, knowing her huſband, though an honeſt, worthy man, to be rather inclined to jealouſy, I never gave

gave the fair one any other token of my attachment, than by buying now and then ſome gingerbread nuts of her, which I never eat; or half a dozen oranges, which I did not want: for, as ſhe is no longer the object of my amorous wiſhes, I will make no ſecret of her place of reſidence; in ſhort, ſhe ſells gingerbread at the foot of Black Fryars Bridge.

This comely matron had ſometimes diſguſted me, by thruſting out an handſome foot and inſtep, disfigured by an awkward man's ſhoe, at the ſide of her baſket. This, however, as it raiſed ſome compaſſion for her humble ſituation, rather operated in her favour. But going by, earlier than uſual, one froſty morning, I ſaw my fair one wrapt up in a horſeman's coat, and ſmoking a long pipe (a ſhort one would have been leſs maſculine) which ſo far diſconcerted me, that

that the miſts of paſſion were immediately diſpelled; and the poor woman loſt both my love and my cuſtom.

From this trifling incident, then, I would take occaſion to exhort thoſe fair ladies in a higher ſphere of life—who, though they do not ſell gingerbread, yet exhibit their charms for the approbation of the beſt, or moſt agreeable purchaſer;—I would exhort them, by all means, to avoid every thing that is bold and maſculine, in their dreſs, their air, their language, and in their whole external deportment.

I am no idolizer of ancient manners; and am rather partial to the times we live in; yet am ſorry to ſee the moſt beautiful part of the creation disfigured by a miſtaken idea of what is beautiful or becoming. They ſeem to confound what is agreeable to their own fancy, with what is likely to pleaſe that of the other ſex; whereas, in general, the very reverſe muſt be the truth of the caſe. If *they* deſpiſe a fribble, why ſhould they imagine that *we* can like a virago? If they are diſguſted with a man that ſeems too well verſed in the myſteries of the toilet, or affects the airs of a lady, why ſhould we be pleaſed with a woman whoſe dreſs is maſculine, and every motion bold and indelicate— and who ambitiouſly diſplays her knowledge of thoſe abſtruſe ſciences, or robuſt exerciſes, which ſeem by nature appropriated to our ſex.

Clariſſa is a charming woman; her perſon, her features, and her manner, are truly feminine. She has a delicate taſte, and a good underſtanding. She is thoroughly accompliſhed in every thing that becomes her ſex; plays on the harpſicord, ſings, and dances uncommonly well. No one decides more judiciouſly

judiciouſly on the merits of our ſeveral dramatic writers, or our moſt celebrated novels. I was afraid to give my opinion of any new production of *that kind*, till I knew that of Clariſſa.

But, in a mixed company, t'other day, ſhe combated and refuted my arguments upon the late peace, and the commutation tax; and entirely demoliſhed my whole ſyſtem of politics.

She might as well have knocked me down, ſworn a great oath, or toſſed off a pot of porter—or even have cocked a Broſely pipe in my face: I ſhould not have been more ſurpriſed, or more diſguſted.

But I have ſince learned, that Clariſſa is not content with being the pretrieſt woman, but is ambitious of being the beſt politician, the beſt hiſtorian, and even the beſt *divine*, in the neighbourhood. This exalts her, in

her

her own imagination; but it diminiſhes and almoſt annihilates her charms in my eye, and in that of every gentleman of my acquaintance.

Great are the privileges, and great is the power of this charming ſex. Every woman, as ſuch, that is not horridly deformed, or in the very decrepitude of old age, is, in ſome meaſure, capable of pleaſing. But, when ſhe diveſts herſelf of every degree of female appearance; when I ſee a lady in a ſcarlet coat, toſſing up her cane, and ſtrutting with a military air,—inſtead of admiring her, I cannot but ſuſpect that this fair Venus is imitating the graces of ſome votary of Mars, who has captivated her fancy. And when I meet a ſtately dowager in a horſeman's coat, and her ſhoulders loaded with a triple cape of cumbrous broad cloth, it raiſes a ſtrong ſuſpicion that the lady has a ſecret attachment to her coachman.

It is very difficult, however, entirely to obſcure or obliterate the charms of youth and beauty. So long as a lady retains the ſlender ſhape and juvenile appearance of an handſome boy, ſhe retains at leaſt a poſſibility of pleaſing in any dreſs. But when an over-grown matron, or full-aged virgin, who perhaps has unfortunately had her features enlarged by the ſmall-pox, or by indulging her appetite—inſtead of giving them a ſoftneſs by an additional quantity of lace and gauze, or other female arts, which modern refinement has invented;—when a lady of this deſcription bundles herſelf up in a coarſe great coat, walks the ſtreet, and ſtumps along with the air of a dragoon, ſhe forfeits her female privileges, and is no longer entitled to our adoration: nay, though none but the most brutal wretch of our sex would dispute the wall, much less insult a woman, however disguised; yet, if she assumed the airs, in such a dress, which she might so justly do in a female one, I should not wonder if a porter or a drayman treated her as one bruiser would treat another, and perhaps give her a black eye, or otherwise disfigure the honours of her face.

So powerful indeed is the feminine character and delicacy of manners to attract that attention and regard which every man is naturally ambitious of shewing to the fair sex; that the beauty, softness, and sensibility of Mary Queen of Scots, incline us to pity her frailties, and palliate her crimes; while the masculine sternness, and unfeeling ſeverity of Elizabeth, make us blind to her virtues, and even execrate her unrelenting cruelty to her captive rival.

In ſhort, if the ladies would ſecure that love, that reſpect, that adoration, which is ſo juſtly due to the lovelieſt part, the ſovereigns, the divinities of this lower creation; let them not exchange the charms of their perſon, the enſigns of their ſovereignty, the attributes of their divinity, for the coarſe habiliments or the robuſt accompliſhments of their admirers, their vaſſals, their devotees, their adorers.

P. S. The good ſenſe of the Engliſh ladies has now almoſt ſuperſeded the neceſſity of theſe reflections.

THE

FEMALE PARTISAN.

" *Delenda est Carthago.*"——CATO's SPEECH.
" These rivals of our sovereignty must be subdued."

WHEN Heav'n first form'd the stately creature, man,
And, to complete creation's wond'rous plan,
Had woman made, and plac'd in due subjection;
Heaven gave her beauty, for her sole protection.
Such beauty sits enthron'd in ———'s eyes,
And wisdom, strength, and sovereign power supplies.

Each

Each nymph, with gentle ſmiles, her point
pursues,
Or with ſoft tears the tyrant man ſubdues.
But, when the fair one mounts the ſtateſman's
box,
And zealouſly contends for P—tt or F—x;
Whether in argument ſhe's wrong or right,
Her manly air puts gentle love to flight.
For politics muſt counteract each charm,
And party rage the brighteſt eyes diſarm.
Her pow'r is loſt amidſt the furious ſtrife;
And the ſoft maid becomes a vixen wife.
Yet, ſay the lady argues well—'tis certain,
Her ſeat of empire lies behind the curtain;
There let the fair one with her ſpouſe debate
The rights of ſubjects, and reform the ſtate.
By female graces they preſerve their ſway;
Their ſmiles, but not their frowns, we pleas'd
obey.

Their greateſt ſtrength in weakneſs women
find,
And, by ſubmiſſion, triumph o'er mankind.

THE
MODERN CESTUS;
OR,
FRIGID ZONE.

VENUS, of old, to make herself look fair,
And give each feature a more lovely air,
Her cestus wore—a kind of magic belt
(Its force in Julia's eyes we oft have felt):
This bound beneath her breasts, or round her arm,
Each amorous god, nay Jove himself, would charm.

Our modern nymphs, resolv'd to live more chaste,
Have bound the zone of virtue round the waist;
And thus, the fort secur'd, do all you can,
They bid defiance to th' assaults of man.
But needless, sure, the zone, thus arm'd with brass,
To guard from force the amazonian lass;
Whose belted, butter-woman's coat must prove
An everlasting antidote to love;
For, sure, on beauty, veil'd in such a shape,
The D–vil himself would ne'er attempt a rape.

THE

VIRAGO.

LAURA, when blooming as the Queen of Love,
With female ſkill your beaŭties you improve;
With flowing curls, with ribands, gauze, or lace,
You ſoften each ſweet feature of your face;
With fineſt lawn your riſing boſom ſhade;
By heavens, my Laura, you're a charming maid!
But when you bind a cravat round your throat,
Strut with a hat and cane, and horſeman's coat,

 Aſſume

Assume each bold, unblushing, manly air,
And dress, and look, and march—*en militaire*;
Indeed, my dear, to say the best we can,
You're a plain woman, not an handsome man.

THE

THE

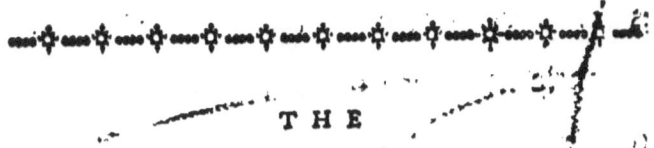

ORIGIN OF GALLANTRY;

OR,

THE FIRST ADULTERER.

A REVERIE.

In a letter from a young lady at Bath, to a young lady of distinction; who, with a female friend, had retired to an elegant cottage, at the foot of Snowdon, in North Wales.

Credite posteri! HOR.

Bath, 10 Jan. 1786.

My dear Parthenia,

I CANNOT forbear giving you an account of an extraordinary person, who has appeared lately in Bath, especially as you will soon have a visit from him; and, as the defcription which I gave him of your romantic fituation, drew from him the following marvellous relation; which indeed appears fo incredible, that I fhould have been almoft afhamed to repeat it, if there were not people filly enough, even in this enlightened age, to give credit to the moft ridiculous improbabilities; of which I need mention no other inftance than that of the Cock-Lane Ghoft, which happened within our memory; and to inveftigate the truth of which, the great Dr. Johnfon was folemnly deputed.

But though the perfon in queftion is fuppofed to have come to Bath in the train of the learned pig, the travelling * *tea-kettle*, and the indecent wax-work; and to have

* A tin houfe built in that fhape.

ſkulked behind when that whole cavalcade was expelled the city, from the jealouſy of the civil government of this place; yet he diſclaims all connection with that ſtrolling party, and came hither upon a more laudable errand, as will appear in the ſequel.

He was introduced to me as a connoiſſeur, by a young gentleman of fortune, who did me the honour to come and ſee ſome drawings, which a friend of mine had made of ſeveral views in your part of North Wales. Upon my ſhewing him the ſketch which ſhe took of your cottage, and mentioning your name, and your ſeemingly romantic plan of life, the ſtranger lifted up his eyes, with a ſort of religious awe, to the cieling— "Heavens!" cries he, "what a jaunt ſhall I have!" On my expreſſing my ſurpriſe at this

this exclamation, he looked round the room, and feeing no one but the gentleman who introduced him, faid; "Madam, I know you have too much fenfe to give credit to every idle tale, and I alfo know fo much of the infidelity of the prefent age, that too many will hardly believe the miracles recorded in their Bible; but, let them trace things up to a certain period (to the univerfal deluge, for inftance, which every appearance of nature confirms) and, if they are not void of all fhame as well as underftanding, they muft be forced to acknowledge a fupernatural interpofition. I have faid thus much upon this fubject, as an introduction to my hiftory.

"You muft know then, Madam," continued he, "that I was born in the land of

Nod,

Nod, ſome centuries before the flood"—— Here, you may ſuppoſe, I ſtared, and ſmiled, with a ſignificant look, upon the gentleman who introduced him.—" Madam," ſays he, " moderate your ſurpriſe, and give me leave to proceed——

" I was born, I ſay, in the land of Nod; and, as my anceſtor Cain was 'the firſt murderer,' I was the *firſt adulterer*; or, in modern language, the firſt man of *gallantry*, who had an affair with a married woman.

" Adultery, though you now make ſo light of it, was then ranked in the next degree of guilt to murder; and my good friend and intimate acquaintance Moſes (the lawgiver of the Jews) many ages after, ſo claſſed it in the decalogue, by divine command.

" I was

"I was ſo much abhorred and deteſted for this abominable crime (continued the ſtranger) that the inhabitants of Nod, though wicked enough in other reſpects, baniſhed me their ſociety; and ſolitude made my life ſo miſerable, that I was often tempted to lay violent hands on myſelf; but was warned by a viſion not to do it, 'as ſuicide was a more heinous crime than that I had been guilty of, being contrary to the firſt law of nature, ſelf-preſervation; and, as it could not be repented of, it could never be forgiven.'

"I was farther informed, that, to puniſh me for my crime, I ſhould be condemned to *live* as long as this world ſhould endure, which was to be ſix thouſand years from its creation, that I might be a witneſs to all the

domeſtic

domeſtic miſery which my example would bring upon mankind. That, as a further puniſhment, I ſhould be in love with every beautiful woman I ſaw, but never ſucceed in my addreſſes; and, if I was wiſe, ſhould never attempt to marry, for fear of a retaliation.

"That, as the only atonement I could make for the miſchief I had occaſioned, I ſhould wander about the world, and do all the good in my power, particularly by warning men againſt the horrid crime of which I had been guilty; and, for that purpoſe, take up my reſidence, in the different ages of the world, in thoſe countries where vices of this kind appeared to be moſt predominant.

"You will naturally wonder," continues

he, "by what means I eſcaped the general deſtruction occaſioned by the flood. This," ſays he, "is the moſt marvellous part of my ſtory; which I will endeavour to explain.

"While Noah and his ſons were building the ark, as I was generally at a loſs for amuſement (the whole world being too corrupt to attend to my admonitions) I was admitted to be a diſtant ſpectator; and often aſſiſted his ſons in falling trees in a neighbouring foreſt.

"From the impious behaviour of Ham, in ridiculing his father, after the flood, you may ſuppoſe he was always wickedly inclined, and was preſerved in the ark merely on account of his father's virtues. In fact, he was infected by the univerſal depravity of the times; and, while he was abſent in

purſuit

pursuit of his intrigues, his amiable wife (lady Ham Noah, as *you* would call a woman of her distinction) to screen her husband from the anger of his father, would supply his place, and assist her brothers in their laborious employment. For the antediluvian ladies, though they had as much beauty, and *real* delicacy, yet were capable of more vigorous personal exertions than our modern ladies of fashion.

" As I could not but endeavour to alleviate the toil of this lady, it naturally produced a considerable degree of intimacy; especially as *her* grief for the infidelity of her husband, and *my* sufferings (with which every one was acquainted) created a mutual sympathy and compassion, approaching nearly to love.

" Neither the lady or myself, however, I am

am convinced, had any thing criminal in our intentions. But I thought it allowable to make uſe of her's and her brothers' partiality in my favour, to effectuate, what I was perſuaded was the will of Providence, the preſervation of my own life.

" For I now perceived in myſelf a drowſineſs, which (as I will explain to you hereafter) brought on a periodical ſleep, of many months, once in about 300 years, by which I was entirely renewed, and reſtored to youth and vigour.

" They therefore readily came into my project, of putting me into a convenient receptacle, in the form of a trunk, and conveying me into a proper ſituation, amongſt the immenſe quantity of provender for the various animals which were to be preſerved in the ark.

" This

" This they must have effectually perform-ed; though I can give no farther account of myself, till my period of sleeping expired, which must have been providentially prolong-ed for some *years*, instead of nine or ten months, my usual time of revification. For, on my descending from the mountains of Ar-menia, where I had lain in my chest, at the bottom of the ark, which the pitch preserved for several ages, on my coming into the valley, on the banks of the Tygris, I found the earth covered with fruits and flowers, in the greatest profusion, and animals of every kind; birds and beasts covering the plains, or sing-ing amongst the branches of the trees.

" On my proceeding still southward, I found yet greater plenty of the richest fruits; and the sun shining in all its glory, gilded the hills

hills and foreſts, and all nature ſeemed reſtored to its primæval beauty. But, alas! I pined in abſolute ſolitude for two or three years, I ſuppoſe, and was ſufficiently puniſhed for the moral evil which I had contributed to bring into the world. When, ſitting, one day, under the ſhade of a palm-tree, I was agreeably ſurprized at the ſight of three or four boys, of about 20 years old, purſuing ſome kind of game amongſt the woods. Rouſed at this ſight, I immediately proceeded in the track from whence they ſeemed to come, when I ſaw a parcel of girls, who ſeemed to be about 14 or 15 years old, elegantly attired, according to the faſhion of that age, and tending ſome flocks of ſheep and herds of cows. They were a little ſurpriſed at ſeeing a perſon of my years, who was a ſtranger to them; but, on my enquiry, ſoon directed me to the head of their family, who was no other than my old acquaintance, Noah's ſecond ſon, Ham.

"They received me with a mixture of ſurpriſe and joy; yet I could not but obſerve that Lady Ham was almoſt paſt her bloom, though I was certain ſhe could not be much above 70 years old: but I ſoon found that ſhe was ſome months advanced in her pregnancy, after having brought near twenty children into the world; for I now was convinced that my ſleep had been prolonged for that number of years.

"But I am running into a tedious detail"——

"Well," ſays his friend, "your detail is not unamuſing — but pray proceed, Mr. Ironſide."

"I could

" I could mention too many previous inſtances of the fatal influence of my example, at Nineveh, Babylon, and the Perſian court; but I ſhall begin with that celebrated one, the Trojan *war*.

" I would have diſſuaded Paris (who conſulted me upon the occaſion) from giving the golden apple (which was to be given 'to the *faireſt*') to Venus, and to have beſtowed it on Minerva; whoſe beauty being of a ſuperior kind, had certainly a better claim to the prize. But he was obſtinate, and accepted Venus's promiſe, of the moſt beautiful woman in the world; which he could not have without the guilt of *adultery*. The conſequence is too well known.

" During the ſiege of Troy, however, I endeavoured to prevent the deſtruction of

that

that noble city. I ran down from the citadel with Laocoon, and would have prevailed on them not to admit the fatal wooden horſe within their walls; but, like Caſſandra's, my advice was rarely attended to.

"I was acquainted with Therſites, who accompanied the Grecian army (for I took every ſhape, in order to do all the good in my power:) he was a droll fellow—the very picture of Voltaire the Frenchman; had as much wit, and knew how to abuſe kings as well as Voltaire. I ſet him on, in hopes of keeping up the quarrel amongſt the Grecian chiefs; but he only got a drubbing for his pains, as Voltaire had like to have done from Frederick the Great.

"But to give you my whole hiſtory, would be to give you the hiſtory of the whole world.—After reſiding, for ſome centuries, in the licentious Eaſtern courts, I attended Alexander in his oriental expedition, and endeavoured to mitigate the horrors of war. I would have ſaved Tyre and Perſepolis; but, as I told you, a great part of my puniſhment was to labour to no purpoſe.

"I had not found my way to Rome till ſome ages after Tarquin's adulterous rape of Lucretia—but I had full employment there for ſeveral ages, under the emperors; and, upon the fall of the empire, paſſed the Alps, and attended the ſeveral courts in the South of Europe.

"I was at Paris (continued the ſtranger) at the maſſacre in 1560; and contrived to ſave the king of Navarre and D. Sully: but, though Henry the Fourth was a good Proteſtant,

Proteſtant, he was a great fornicator; and his example encouraged every ſpecies of lewdneſs. And the French court found me ſufficient employment during the minority of Lewis the Thirteenth, and great part of the laſt century.

" But, on the reſtoration of Charles the Second to the crown of England, my duty called me thither; where I remained till the death of that monarch. I ſhould then have returned to France, had it not been for the revocation of the edict of Nantz the preceding year, and the perſecution of the Proteſtants which enſued; for, as I was known to be a zealous friend to truth, and of courſe to the reformed religion, I thought myſelf much ſafer in England. Here accordingly I reſided, till after the Revolution; and, having been introduced, by a particular friend, to the great earl of Devonſhire, I ſpent ſome time at his beautiful ſeat at Chatſworth; and attended him to the county meeting at Derby, when he made a ſpeech, which brought over a majority of the freeholders to the prince of Orange. He told them, "that to reſiſt a king, who ruled according "to the *laws*, was treaſon; but, when a king "endeavoured to ſubvert the laws and reli- "gion of his country, he forfeited all claim "to the allegiance of his ſubjects, and "might lawfully be reſiſted."

"During the reign of the virtuous queen Anne, I returned to France; but came into England again ſoon after the acceſſion of George the Firſt, and have continued here to this day."

But,

But, not to tire my dear Parthenia with his general hiſtory, I will come to the point, and the intention of this long letter.

" The Engliſh ladies," ſaid he, " in this reign, though perhaps not worſe than in ſome other periods, have been leſs cautious in their conduct; and women of acknowledged virtue, leſs ſcrupulous in mixing with thoſe of dubious characters; I have endeavoured, therefore," continued he, " by various methods, to warn the innocent againſt the ſeducing influence of vicious examples. I attended," ſays he, " though unknown, that beautiful and ſenſible character the preſent D——— of D———, in the zenith of her charms and bridal ſplendor, and anxiouſly watched over her in her nocturnal routs and midnight revels; to which, urged on by youthful ſpirits, and the force of faſhion, her Grace ſo intrepidly approached: but I ſoon found," ſaid he, " my guardian care was altogether unneceſſary; as I ſaw that her virtue was as impregnable, as her beauty was irreſiſtible.

" I would have prevented her Grace," continued he, " from ſullying the celeſtial bloom of female delicacy, by randying with the mob in Covent-Garden, at the Weſtminſter election—but the impetuoſity of a female partiſan is more ungovernable, than the fury of a lioneſs in the paroxyſm of amorous deſire.

" I have been pretty conſtantly employed," continued he, " for ſome years, in your metropolis, as I ſaid before, in guarding againſt the frailty of the ſex; but, upon the abdication of the late ' comptroller of

' your

'your pleasures' at Bath, I thought it of more consequence to attend this fountain-head of gallantry; especially, as I heard a party was forming to restore a late monarch, who had been banished for the same crime of which I so unfortunately set the example. I succeeded tolerably well, in getting two gentlemen of honour elected; though, as the chastity of your wives and daughters is of so much importance to the welfare of the community, I would have recommended an amiable Italian, from whose example there could have been no possibility of danger."

He now returned to his remarks on your retired situation, and his intention of visiting you. He had not a doubt, he said, but that you had been bred up in the strictest principles of virtue and honour, as he could apply to your's what he had heard remarked of another noble family; 'That all the wo-'men were virtuous, and all the men were 'valiant.'—" But," continues he, " a young lady is in more danger in ſolitude, than in all the gaiety and diſſipation of public life. Many a young woman," he ſaid, " who had withſtood, or capriciouſly rejected, the ad-dreſſes of a worthy man of her own rank, has afterwards repented, and been drawn in by ſome inſignificant or worthleſs object, when her ſequeſtered ſituation has precluded her from having a better choice. In ſoli-tude, a lady is in danger from every male creature that comes in her way—her muſic-maſter, her hair-dreſſer, or even her own do-meſtics, may prove dangerous to her vir-tuous reſolutions."

I looked

I looked grave at these indelicate insinuations; which he perceived, and, recovering himself, said, "that his imagination had transported him into the Oriental and Asiatic courts, and suggested the strict cautions and regulations of their Harams and their Seraglios."

I then mentioned your manner of life and your amusements; and shewed him your elegant poetical compositions, and the exquisite productions of your pencil. He was in raptures of astonishment; but still insisted, that, although those amusements might please for a time, yet the natural passions would resume their *just* claims; and, when suppressed in youth, their proper season, would bud forth in the winter of life:—hence we frequently see old bachelors, in their grand climacteric, marry their maids; and there have been inſtances, though very few, even of old ladies eſpouſing their footmen.

"In ſhort," continued the ſtranger, "without the leaſt apprehenſion for young ladies of ſuch a character as your friends, I find myſelf impelled by mere curioſity to make them a viſit. I ſhall contrive to ſearch out, with diſcretion, their connections; ſhall attend them unperceived in their evening walks; enquire into their domeſtic œconomy; and, if poſſible, get introduced to their converſation, and, perhaps, be entertained with more of the elegant productions of their pens and their pencils."—Here he pauſed, and ſeemed wrapt in meditation.

That you may be upon your guard, therefore, I muſt inform you, that he has nothing

nothing very particular in his appearance—he looks very old, and is very thin; but, so far from being any ways infirm, he is not only active, but rapid in his motions; and says himself, 'that he can walk, talk, read, and write, faster than most men in Europe.'

He dresses very plain, much like a senator of the last age.—I could not forbear asking him a few obvious questions; particularly, how he could preserve life for so many generations? (not that I believed he had really done so, you may be sure.) He said, that by a *strict* regimen, and constant exercise, begun in youth and rigidly observed, most men might preserve their lives to one hundred years.

He added, however, (as I hinted before)

that about the end of every century he found himſelf gradually ſeized by a more than ordinary drowſineſs and tendency to doze; upon which occaſions he found a ſort of divine impulſe or inſtinct (like that by which the bats and beetles are probably actuated) to ſeek ſome unfrequented cave or ſubterraneous receſs, where he uſually ſlept for nine months, and then came forth from the womb of the earth, as freſh as a young child, with a new ſet of teeth, hair, &c.

Here I could no longer ſuppreſs a loud laugh; and, conſidering him as a foreigner, "Ah! Monſieur," cried I, "vous badinez! —you are pleaſed to rally us." "Madam," replied he, with a ſerious air, "I have not mentioned a ſingle circumſtance but what I *ſaw* with my own eyes—though I confeſs it

was

was with my 'mind's eye,' or imagination —in a kind of reverie, between ſleeping and waking—this very morning. If it is a fiction, it was really impreſſed on my fancy with the force of *reality*; and I ſhould not have related it to you, if I had not thought it has a *moral* tendency." The ſtranger then took his leave; and you will rejoice to have me do the ſame.—Believe me, my dear Parthenia, your and Serena's affectionate friend, —— ———.

P. S. He added, that in different ages of the world he had been miſtaken for ſeveral myſterious characters; as, for the wandering Jew, &c. &c.; and in the laſt age, for the Turkiſh Spy. He confeſſed that he had been intimate with the ce-

lebrated

lebrated author of Junius's Letters; but when he proſtituted his wit, in ſo ſhamefully confounding the moſt worthy and reſpectable characters with the moſt abandoned, merely to pleaſe a party, he renounced all acquaintance and connexion with him. I at firſt ſuſpected this might have been the unborn doctor, Count Caglioſtro; but recollected he was at that time in the Baſtile.

TAXOLOGY;

OR,

JOHN BULL

AND HIS

COUSIN WILLIAM.

——— Fugiant *examina Taxos.* VIRG.

" Let our *swarms* of manufacturers be exempted from
" taxes."

ADVERTISEMENT.

THE Author of the following Trifle is too insignificant to list himself under any party; and declares himself absolutely incapable of deciding which is right: But he has always thought it his duty to submit to the decisions of the Legislature, *even upon the principle of an heathen poet.*

"—— Vir bonus est quis?
"Qui consulta patrum, qui leges juraque servat."
Hor.

"*Things are not right."—What's that to you or me?*
Good subjects must *obey the pow'rs that be.*

TAXOLOGY.

Quousque tandem, Gulielme, abutêre patientiâ nostrâ? quem ad finem sese effrænata jactabit audacia? Cic.

"HOW long then, O thou dæmon of Taxation! how long wilt thou abuse our patience? what bounds wilt thou prescribe to thy enormous exactions on this devoted land? But whither shall we fly then from thy incessant persecutions? if we go into France, thou art there; if we pass into Holland, thou art there also; if we fly to the utmost parts of the East, even there thy

thy rapacious claws will ſeize us! or if we croſs the Atlantic, thou rageſt with tenfold fury in the Utopian ſtates of America!"

Thus I went on, profanely murmuring, punning, and quibbling upon the rapid increaſe of our Taxes; and added, that we muſt ſurely return again to our berries and acorns, and drink of the yet-unexciſed limpid ſtreams—when, in the midſt of my ſeditious exclamations, an old ſoldier, who had loſt an arm and a leg in the ſervice, came towards the door: "Well, ſoldier," ſaid I, "you are but in wretched plight; however, you have no land-tax or houſe-tax to pay." "No, Maſter, I wiſh I had!"—"Nor ſervant's-tax, nor coach-tax, nor horſe-tax, nor even ſhop-tax, to pay, I ſuppoſe?"—"Ah! Maſter," ſays he, "there you touch the very ſtring that vibrates to my heart!—That is the height of my ambition; to keep a little *ſhop* in a country town, where my wife might ſell tobacco, and ſugar, and powder and ſhot, and ſuch like; and I, with my one arm and my ſtump could knit cabbage-nets—and I would gladly pay *twenty* ſhillings a year for my ſhop-tax."

"Well," ſaid I (with a ſixpence in my hand) where did you loſe your limbs, ſoldier?"

"Where? Maſter! why, in fighting againſt the *rebellious* Americans."

"Why do you call your brethren and fellow-ſubjects *rebels?*" ſaid I (putting up my ſixpence); "they fought bravely for their liberty, rather than be *taxed* as we are."—"Why, Sir, for that very reaſon I call them

rebels;

rebels; if they were our fellow-ſubjects, why ſhould not they pay *taxes* as well as the reſt of the king's ſubjects?"

"Well," ſaid I, "go to the door, and get ſomething to eat and drink."

Upon conſidering the affair more coolly, however, I began to reflect with myſelf; Why do I pay houſe-tax? Why, becauſe I have a houſe to live in.—Why do I pay coach-tax? Becauſe I have a coach to ride in.—I have a horſe to carry me, ſervants to wait on me, and am *ſecured* by the *government* in the quiet enjoyment of all theſe conveniencies of life.—The ſoldier has loſt his limbs, in maintaining what he thought the rights of his country—I only pay about an hundredth part of my poſſeſſions to ſecure the reſt.

Having then ſettled the affair with myſelf and with my ſteward, I went to prepare for my journey to London, the next day. Here I began to purſue the ſame train of reflection.—What am I going to town for? Why, to ſee the pictures at the royal exhibition, or to hear the muſic in commemoration of Handel.—But, are pictures or muſic amongſt the *neceſſaries* of life? No.—Are they any part of the *conveniences* of life? No.—I have money then, it ſeems, even for *ſuperfluities*, notwithſtanding our enormous taxes.

When I got to town, I could not but obſerve to a friend, that luxury and ſplendor ſeemed to be increaſed, in more than a duplicate proportion, ſince I was laſt in London. "Yes," replied he, "towards the court end of the metropolis, I believe, it may."

I ſoon

I ſoon after dined with a friend in the city, who is a zealous oppoſer of the ſhop-tax; and our firſt health, after dinner, was "*Confuſion to the projectors of it.*"

I obſerved, however, that neither my friend nor his wife had abated any thing of their uſual ſplendor, on account of our new taxes, and could not forbear rallying them upon the occaſion. I applied the ſame teſt as in my own caſe; and aſked them, for inſtance, whether ſilver ſauce-boats, ſilver ſkewers, or a ſilver trowel to cut pudding, were amongſt the *neceſſaries* of life? No.—Are they amongſt the *conveniences?* The ſame utenſils, of cheaper materials, might be equally *convenient.*—Well then, continued I, notwithſtanding the *oppreſſive* taxes, which we complain of, we

have

have ſtill money enough for *ſuperfluities*, I find.

In ſhort, inſtead of that imaginary diſtreſs and poverty which I had apprehended, I found, in the metropolis, extravagance and luxury prevail amongſt all ranks and deſcriptions of people.

Whence then is this outcry of oppreſſion and arbitrary impoſition of burthens, particularly on the lower claſs of ſubjects? Why, partly from ignorance; and partly, I believe, from the intereſted ſuggeſtions of diſappointed partiſans, who teach the multitude to complain of evils which they hardly feel; or to murmur at thoſe trifling reſtraints, which, for the public benefit, it has been found neceſſary to impoſe upon their uſual indulgence.

Few

Few people reflect how intimately the happiness of every *individual* is connected with that of the *community*, and therefore are unwilling to contribute the least particle of their private property, even for the preservation of their country from ruin.

Having reflected on these particulars with coolness and impartiality, I sate down to a dish of Commutation Tea with some friends of the minister; and, from execrating the taxes, we soon agreed, that they were absolutely necessary to our existence as a people, and by no means insupportable or oppressive.

"*My murmurs ceas'd: I too submitted;*
And, like my ancestors, was * bitted. GAY.

* Others read,
" And, like my *company*, was *Pitt-ed*."
That is, from being partial to Mr. F—x, I became a friend to Mr. P-tt. Judicet lector.

TAXOLOGY;

OR,

JOHN BULL and his COUSIN WILL.

"Invitum qui ſervat, idem facit occidenti." HOR.

"'Tis much the ſame, at once to kill,
"As ſave a man againſt his will."

THOUGH long by numerous foes op-
preſt,
When Britain proudly rears her creſt,
And luxury yet more powerful waxes,
Can we complain of grievous taxes?
Or talk of national diſtreſſes?
View then our furniture, our dreſſes;
Yon ſplendid equipage behold!
With ſilver deck'd, and burniſh'd gold.

With Florio dine; observe what ſtate!
His viands, wines, and ſhew of plate!
His ſervants deck'd with richeſt laces,
And wanton plenty in their faces!
Ah! what would many a Frenchman give
To live as your domeſtics live!
But Engliſhmen, not over humble,
Still claim their privilege—to grumble.
Like good John Bull, who held, of late,
With couſin Will, this grand debate;
And, though he needed his aſſiſtance,
To every plan made ſtrong reſiſtance.
John Bull, who'd liv'd for half a cent'ry,
Careſs'd by all the neighbouring gentry,
An honeſt, hearty, boon-companion,
Who'd eat and drink, or fight with any one;
And oft, to gain a ſtick or ſtraw,
Would boldly ſtand a ſuit at law *;

* See Swift's Hiſtory of John Bull.

At length, by thoughtlefs diffipation,
And many an idle litigation,
Poor John, the fpendthrift's ufual fate,
Had deeply mortgag'd his eftate.
His fervants cheated him; his fteward,
In league with all his tradefmen, drew hard:
Each knave, in his refpective poft,
Contending who fhould fleece him moft.

And now his debts came in apace,
And ruin ftar'd him in the face:
When a young counfel, his relation,
Vex'd at fuch mal-adminiftration,
Engag'd (by his good kinfman's leave)
In time, his fortune to retrieve,
If John would, like a prudent man,
Concur in his falubrious plan.

John faid, he gladly would fubmit
To what his fage young friend thought fit.

First, then, your debts to liquidate,
Which eat ſo deep in your eſtate;
For this, good Sir, you muſt ('tis plain)
A ſtrict *œconomy* maintain.
Why, yes, quoth John, that's very true;
'Tis what I would be glad to do.
Well, ere to greater things we come,
We muſt ſet matters right at home.
Your houſekeeping retrench at once,
All ſuperfluities renounce;
In every article ſpend leſs,
In *meat*, in *drink*, in dogs, in dreſs.
Hold! hold! quoth John—zounds, Sir, d'ye think
To ſtint me in my *meat* and *drink*?
I'd have you know, young man, John Bull
Muſt always have his belly-full;
And, though no epicure or glutton,
I can't dine every day on mutton.

And then my *hounds!* my health requires;
Sure! I may hunt, like other 'ſquires.
And, why not *dreſs*, on fit occaſions?
At race-time, or at quarter-ſeſſions.
Not that on dreſs I vainly doat, Sir,
But I *muſt* have a decent coat, Sir.
In ſhort, for money let the king come,
I'll not give up my annual income:
So, if you'll pay my debts, you *may*;
But, faith! I'll have it my own way.
I can't turn milkſop on a ſudden,
Or dine on garden-ſtuff and pudding.
I'll drink ſtrong beer, and give up wine,
And on *three* diſhes *only* dine;
And if all theſe reſources fail,
I'll be content, and go to jail.
 Well, Sir, purſue your own wiſe plan;
Yet ſtill I'll *do* the beſt I can,

(Though you diflike what I am doing)
To fave your *family* from ruin.
And, fhould my project once fucceed
(Of which I've not a doubt indeed,
And that, at length, I fhall content ye)
You'll live again in peace and plenty.——

Such are the clamours of the nation,
Againft young P–tt's adminiftration.
We own, that money *muft* be found,
Yet grudge e'en fixpence in the pound.
Let thofe, who *will*, the burthen bear,
So *we* 're not forc'd to pay our fhare.
E'en thofe who praife our patriot meafures,
Will not confent to tax their *pleafures*.

The gambler thinks it curfed hard,
To have a tax on every card;
For, fure, no burthen fhould be laid
On *tools* effential to *their trade!*

Is't

Is't thus great Chatham's ſon advances
The produce of the ſtate's finances?
  The man of fortune is unwilling
To pay a land-tax of one ſhilling:
But, what he deems a great deal worſe, is
To pay for ſervants, coach, and horſes;
And, blind to what his cook within does,
Curſes the *tax* upon his windows;
Envies the cobler in his ſtall,
Too *needy* to be tax'd at all.
  The mercer ſpruce, an eſſenc'd fop,
Won't pay a farthing for his ſhop:
Augment the *land-tax*, if you pleaſe,
So he can live in pomp and eaſe.
  The haberdaſher's wife, ſo friſky,
On Sundays, mounted in her whiſky,
For our diſtreſs cares not a louſe,
But whirls it to her country houſe.

"What is the nation's debt to me?—
I'll have my rout—and public tea."

Thus luxury, rise in every station,
Regardless of a sinking nation,
Still thwarts each plan for reformation.

Yet P–tt, unmov'd by opposition,
Acts like an honest state physician;
Resolv'd and faithful to his trust,
By med'cines safe, by measures just,
Proceeds by steps, though slow, yet sure,
To heal our wounds, and work our cure.
Applauded by the virtuous few,
Convinc'd the course he steers is true,
He slights the senseless, clamorous crew;
And, 'spite of all their noise and pudder,
Unless compell'd to quit the rudder,
Will manfully his foes withstand,
And guide the vessel safe to land.

Faxit Deus! Sept. 1785.

THE

CHARACTERS

OF

CÆSAR AND CATO;

Imitated from SALLUST's Catil. War.

ON reading of and considering the many great atchievements of the English nation, both at home and abroad, by sea and by land; their wars carried on against the most powerful states; great fleets subdued by an inferior force; battles fought; great armies routed, and victories gained, by an handful of men; it appeared evident to me, that these great exploits were to be attributed to the diſtinguiſhed abilities, or extraordinary courage, of a *few* great men *.

But, ſince the nation has become ſo corrupt, and enervated by luxury and indolence, the grandeur and great reſources of the ſtate have, in their turn, ſupported it, amidſt the blunders and miſmanagement of their commanders, and their ruling powers.

For, during the later period of our hiſtory, England (worn out, as it were, with bearing ſo numerous an offspring) has produced hardly one great man. Yet there have flouriſhed, within my memory, two gentlemen of uncommon abilities, though of different characters; Mr. Charles F–x, and Mr. William P–tt; whom, as the occaſion offers itſelf, I am unwilling to paſs by in ſilence;

* From the time of the Black Prince, by Cecil, the Duke of Marlborough, and the great Lord Chatham.

but

but will delineate their characters to the beſt of my power, and exhibit them in as candid a light as their different manners and diſpoſitions will admit.

Theſe two gentlemen, then, in their family, in their age, and in their eloquence, were nearly equal. Their greatneſs of mind, their ambition, and their renown, were ſimilar: but in other reſpects, there was a conſiderable difference between them.

Mr. F–x was greatly extolled for his generous acts and munificence: Mr. P–tt, by the integrity of his life, was eſteemed truly great and reſpectable. The former was celebrated for his mild and compaſſionate temper: The ſeverity of his virtue added dignity to the latter. Mr. F–x, by beſtowing favours, by aſſiſting his friends, and by pardoning his enemies, became extremely popular: Mr. P–tt, by giving no bribes, and by granting no pensions, gained great reputation. In the one, there was a refuge for the miserable; in the other, sure vengeance on the guilty. The easy, pliable temper of the former; the inflexible resolution of the latter, was applauded.

In short, Mr. F–x was indefatigable, vigilant; intent on the service of his friends, and negligent of his own private affairs. He would refuse them nothing, which was worth their acceptance. Yet, he was ambitious of acquiring great power; and wished for some extraordinary emergency, where his great abilities might display themselves to advantage.—Mr. P–tt, on the other hand, was studiously modest, decent, and of a rigid

œconomy

œconomy in the public adminiſtration. He vied not with the rich in oſtentation, or with party zealots in faction; but with the active, in the exertion of his talents; with the modeſt, in ſobriety of manners; with the uncorrupt, in juſtice and integrity. He was more ſolicitous to be really good, than to appear ſo. Thus, the leſs he ſeemed to aim at glory, the more effectually he obtained it.

20 Feb. 1786.

PARLIA-

PARLIAMENTARY REFORM.

PROSAIC TRUTHS.

YE patriots rouſe! excite a general ſtorm.;
And *force* a Parliamentary *Reform!*—
Yet, in your noble project's execution,
Improve, not *change*, our envied conſtitution;
Whoſe gradual progreſs, trac'd through different ages,
Proves it the maſter-piece of wiſeſt ſages;
So nicely balanc'd, that, what oft is ſeen,
The ſlighteſt change may ſtop the whole machine.

First,

First, then, ye great Utopian projectors!
Reform the morals of your poor *electors*;
Teach them by industry a fund to gain,
And, by a frugal management, maintain
Their future lives: nor on base bribes depend;
For luxury soon in poverty *must* end.
Let no one vote, unless who freely swears,
He's not been seven times drunk in seven long
years;
This will contract the *number*, not the *weight*,
Of these unhewn supporters of the state.
But let th' elected an example give,
How they and their constituents ought to live;
And, if some festal tide the House release
From weightier cares, and public business cease;
Like D——, leave routs and gambling in the
lurch,
And shew your faces at your borough church;
Amuse

Amuſe yourſelves amidſt th' untutor'd throng,
Teach them what duties to their ſtate belong;
Nor feed, but check, th' exceſs thoſe ſeaſons bring,
Teach them their God to fear—to love their king.

Reform this curſed life of diſſipation,
And live a model to a ſenſeleſs nation;
Like ſober citizens of ancient Rome,
Commence a reformation firſt at home;
Or Engliſhmen, of former ages, "* knock
" Your ſervants up, and riſe at ſix o'clock;"
Who're now to vice and drunkenneſs a prey,
While you thus watch by night, and ſleep by day:

* Pope's Tranſlation of Horace.

Breakfaſt at eight; nor bluſh to hear it ſaid,
" The Houſe is *met*;" not going now to *bed*.
No longer gratify each lawleſs paſſion;
Be temperate, juſt, bring *Chaſtity* in faſhion;
Check Vice and Luxury; true to Virtue's cauſe;
And let your *lives* exemplify your *laws*.
Diſcharge the uſeleſs train of idle knaves,
Who drain your wealth, and force you to be ſlaves.
Nor let your ſteeds, for uſe, not grandeur, born,
Conſume Heaven's choiceſt bleſſing, wholeſome corn,
Deſign'd to feed th' induſtrious, labouring poor,
Who *claim* ſubſiſtence—though they aſk no more.
Live within bounds, nor dread the power of kings;
Places and penſions will be harmleſs things.

If perjur'd members dare to bribe, don't
ſpare 'em,
Spare private property: nor think Old Sarum,
Or P—tersfield, or Am—ſham, e'er ſent,
Leſs independent men to parliament,
Than thoſe more populous towns, whoſe venal
tribes
A Nabob purchaſes, and intereſt bribes.
In ſhort, let individuals mend their ways,
And parliaments will ſoon ſee happier days.
Thus may we hope political ſalvation,
The *Houſe* will need no other *reformation*.

A COA-

A COALITION,

"DEVOUTLY TO BE WISH'D *."

WHAT! more removes! already change
the dishes!
Another scramble for the loaves and fishes!—
Ah! where are faith and public spirit fled?
Is all true patriotism with Chatham dead?
Who now regards this once-respected nation?
Whence can we hope political salvation?
No system form'd, but for the present hour!
No plan, but how to raise ourselves to pow'r!

* "Consensus omnium bonorum." Cic.

But,

But, though eternal ſquabbles vex the land,
And leave all public buſineſs at a ſtand;
While diſcord thus the Britiſh name diſgraces,
Yet Whigs *join* Tories to ſecure their places.
Why then not do, what you're convinc'd is right,
To ſave the realm, all honeſt men unite?
Each lend a hand, to better our condition,
And Heav'n ſhall bleſs the glorious *Coalition*!

29 Dec. 1783.

LIBERTY.

LIBERTY.

IN theſe bleſt iſles, where jocund nymphs and ſwains
In peace and ſafety range the rural plains;
Where all men boldly ſpeak, and act, and write,
And on king, lords, and commons vent their ſpite;
Where all are govern'd by impartial laws,
What mean theſe volunteers in freedom's cauſe?
Why thus inſult the nation's common ſenſe,
With wrongs unfelt, and "undue *influence?*"
To rouſe the mob, theſe patriots of an hour
Would level church and ſtate, till they're in pow'r;

Then

Then they applaud what they condemn'd before:
Let them be tyrants, *ſlavery* is no more.
They to themſelves, not *liberty*, are friends,
Would *ſerve* the public, for their private ends.
Thus fools are flatter'd by the craft of knaves,
Our *rage* for liberty—will make us ſlaves.

ENNUI;

OR,

SOLITARY REFLECTIONS AT AN INN.

WHATEVER appearance of levity I may ſometimes exhibit, or with whatever ſports of fancy I may have endeavoured to amuſe my leiſure hours, I find myſelf, when alone, a prey to *Ennui*, or a diſtaſte of life; and far from happy, at leaſt, in my preſent ſtate.

I let my thoughts range abroad, to the utmoſt extent of my knowledge; but I find nothing on which they can repoſe themſelves,

ſelves, as a ſufficient ground of conſolation. The confidential friends and ſprightly companions of my youth are, long ſince, either gone into the inviſible world, or entirely ſeparated from me in remote parts of the kingdom. And in thoſe later acquaintance, whom mere vicinity, or other accidental circumſtances, have thrown in my way, I find a cold reſerve, or formal civility, ill calculated to ſupply the place of the warm and unſuſpecting openneſs of my earlier friendſhips.

The viſionary plans of happineſs, of learning, or of fame, which dazzled my imagination in the morning of life, are vaniſhed, like the baſeleſs fabric of a dream. My ſolitary amuſement, or public diverſions, no longer pleaſe—even the ſtated employment of my life, not having been very successfully pursued, is irksome on the recollection.

If I turn my reflections towards my domestic comforts—the dear partner of my joys and sorrows, ruffled by œconomical concerns, and by frequent ill-health, though not less beloved, or less studious to alleviate my anxiety, is less capable of effecting it.

My children, whom I love beyond every thing, are yet fresh sources of my solicitude, as the prospect of their future success in life seems very precarious; some of them appearing less attentive to procure a comfortable establishment in the world, than to grasp at every phantom of present pleasure; which must probably end in a habit of disſipation, and a diſlike of, and inaptitude for, any uſeful employment.

Similar to mine are probably the reflections of thouſands, even of the happieſt part of mankind, at different periods of their lives; for which forlorn ſtate of things this whole world affords no adequate reſource.

But is this then the neceſſary lot of humanity? Was the ſovereign of this lower creation deſtined by nature merely to dreſs and undreſs; to eat, drink, and ſleep, and to toil, for ſixty years, and produce a race of beings, like himſelf, to ſucceed to the ſame toils; or, at beſt, to cultivate his faculties, and ſtore his mind with an endleſs variety of ſcience, and curious ſpeculations, and then ſink into eternal oblivion?

My reaſon aſſures me, beyond a poſſibility of doubt, that this world, and its inhabitants, were made by a wiſe and good being, who would not ſuffer his creatures to be deluded by ſuch conſtant hopes and aſpirations after a more perfect and a more durable ſtate of felicity, if thoſe hopes were never to be gratified.

Though I myſelf, then, ought to reſt ſatisfied, yet if I ſhould ſay, that religion, and REVEALED RELIGION, alone, can afford a complete and adequate conſolation for the miſeries of life, I ſhould perhaps ſpeak unintelligibly to many of thoſe unhappy gentlemen who, having at an early age exhauſted the whole ſtock of ſenſual pleaſures, are moſt frequently expoſed to this Ennui, this Tædium Vitæ, or diſguſt of life; and have ſeldom troubled themſelves about religion, either natural or revealed.

Certain it is, however, that when we contemplate the Deity in a cold philoſophical light, and addreſs ourſelves to him merely as the creator and governor of the univerſe, we are loſt in the immenſity of the divine nature. The imagination ranges through the boundleſs regions of ſpace and time, like the dove in the univerſal deluge, and cannot find even an olive-branch to ſpeak *peace* to the ſoul; we feel nothing to intereſt the heart and engage the affections.

But when we conſider the Deity in the light in which our ſacred writings repreſent him, as, "in ſundry times and in divers manners," converſing with and inſtructing his creatures in their duty, by his prophets, and

and other holy men; particularly by his last great prophet, the prophet of Nazareth (though, if we allow him no higher title, the Scripture certainly makes use of unintelligible language): when, I say, we consider God in this endearing and familiar light; the gloom that surrounds us is immediately dispersed; we address him as a friend and benefactor; we find our hopes encouraged and our love inflamed. And when we contemplate the amiable character of Jesus of Nazareth; if we give but the lowest degree of credit to his promises and pretensions, much more, if we firmly believe (what every careful enquirer must believe) that he was charged with a commission from heaven, to proclaim the pardon of our sins, and to reconcile us to our offended Creator, by a vicarious atonement for the violated laws of his moral government; and if we would accept him as "*the captain of our ſalvation,*" to re-conduct us to the company of our loſt friends and relations, and "to the ſpirits of good men made more perfect," in a ſtate of endleſs felicity;—ſuppoſing, I ſay, that we think his pretenſions entitled to a ſufficient degree of credibility, this will do more towards a cure of our *diſguſt of life*, and towards rendering us tolerably happy, than all that this world can afford beſides.

To a perſon benighted, and wandering in the dark, in a ſtrange country, how comfortable is the glimmering even of a ruſh-light from a diſtant cottage!

How gladly then ſhould we behold the leaſt gleam of ſunſhine amidſt this gloomy

atmoſphere!

atmosphere! with what rapture receive the slightest degree of intelligence from those regions beyond the grave,

"—*From whose bourn no traveller returns.*"

I myself cannot doubt of the truth of revelation; and I will not attempt to prove its credibility to those into whose hands these trifling reflections may happen to fall; as it has been so often done, by the most learned men, and the greatest philosophers, both laity and clergy, in every part of Europe *.

But there is one argument, though less striking at first sight, which has always operated most forcibly on me; that Saint Paul,

* Grotius, Le Clerc, Milton, Newton, Locke, Conybeare, Lord Lyttelton, &c. &c.

when writing to ſo polite and intelligent a people as the Corinthians then were, and in ſeveral other of his epiſtles, frequently mentions the various *miraculous powers*, as *then ſubſiſting* in the church *, with as much confidence that they had been eye-witneſſes to them, and at the ſame time with as much indifference, as he ſpeaks of his having left his cloak and his parchments at Troas.

Now, ſuppoſe any one in this age, when writing to a friend, were to obſerve, " You know, Sir, there are in our church diverſities of *ſupernatural* operations, and different methods of raiſing ghoſts: one b-ſh-p does it by talking Latin to them; another, by repeating Hebrew verſes to them; a third, by preaching to them; and a fourth, by writing

* 1 Cor. xii. &c. &c.

political

political pamphlets againſt them; yet all theſe ſeveral operations are performed by the *ſame* ſupernatural powers;—and that any one, who had liſtened to theſe ghoſts, never laughed, got drunk, kept miſtreſſes, or did any thing immoral afterwards as long as he lived"—Any one, I ſay, that ſhould write thus to his friend, in an age when we know there is no ſuch thing exiſting amongſt us, would be thought as mad as the knight of La Mancha, or as Lord Peter*, or any other lord in the three kingdoms.

In ſhort, he that gets over or doubts of the hiſtorical facts on which the truth of revelation is founded †, ſuch a one may doubt

* See Swift's Tale of a Tub.

† I mean, after a candid and cloſe examination; for thoſe who have acuteneſs enough to raiſe objections, ought to take pains to anſwer them.

whether Cæſar conquered Pompey at the battle of Pharſalia, created himſelf perpetual dictator, and was afterwards aſſaſſinated by Brutus and Caſſius in the ſenate-houſe.

5 Aug. 1772.

P. S. This ſlight ſketch is inſerted, in hopes, that in this ſuperficial age—when, as Dr. Johnſon obſerves (leſs juſtly of Scotland than moſt other nations) learning is diſtributed like bread in a ſiege, when every one has a mouthful, and no one fills his belly—ſome one may be tempted to inquire further into the truth of our religion *.

* Since this was ſent to the preſs, I ſee Dr. Beattie, under the patronage of the excellent Biſhop of Cheſter, has publiſhed two ſmall volumes in 12mo, which ſeem well calculated for this purpoſe.

COMPLIMENTS, &c.

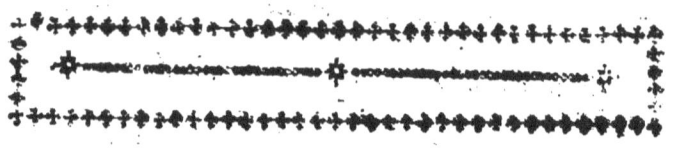

MARTIAL. B. i. Ep. 26.

IMITATED.

" Est tibi tandem, &c."

To CHRISTOPHER A—STY, Esq.

HOW long, my friend, shall thus [illegible] remain
The love[illegible], hopeful offspring of your brain?
How long through all the town thus w[illegible]
Collect, unite them in one [illegible]
They long have gain[illegible] your [illegible]
plaudit;
A[illegible] grav[illegible] Oxford [illegible]

MARTIAL, B. i. Ep. 26,

IMITATED.

" *Ede tuos tandem, &c.*"

To CHRISTOPHER A—STY, *Esq.*

HOW long, my friend, ſhall thus forlorn remain
The lovely, hopeful offspring of your brain?
How long through all the town thus wildly roam?
Collect, unite them in one decent tome.
They long have gain'd your native Cam's applauſe,
And brav'd e'en * Oxford Johnſon's rigid laws.

* Noſtri ſenes.

Fame

Fame ſtands attendant with her wreath of bays,
Proud to augment your well-earn'd meed of
 praiſe ;
Why not admit the goddeſs at your door ?
Why wait for glory till it's heard no more ?
Let your own works your own laſt poliſh claim,
Nor truſt to your executors your fame.
Too late, alas ! the brighteſt honours come,
* Which friendſhip's hand inſcribes upon our
 tomb.

* Cineri gloria ſera venit.

Plato's Epigram on Aristophanes.

THE Muses long had ſought, in various places,
A ſpot to build a temple to the Graces:—
A ſhrine, where pleas'd the Graces might reſide,
The breaſt of Ariſtophanes ſupplied.

ON THE

DEATH

OF

LESBIA's SPARROW*.

From CATULLUS.

"*Lugete, O Veneres Cupidinesque, &c.*"

WEEP, all ye little sportive Loves!
Weep, Venus, with thy plaintive doves!
Each gentle soul, of feelings fine,
The sad procession weeping join!
For ah! my Lesbia's Sparrow's dead,
All joy is with her darling fled!

* See an elegant print on this subject, by Angelica Kauffman.

Her

Her Sparrow Lesbia wont to prize
More than her own dear lovely eyes!
And sure it was the * *sweetest* creature!
All love, and play, and pure good-nature.
Their mutual fondness for each other,
Surpass'd the infant's and its mother.
He never from her bosom stray'd,
But round her hopp'd, and † chirp'd and play'd.

Yet now he's gone " to that dark bourne,
" From which no mortal things return."
Ah! woe betide that gloomy coast,
Where all things fair and good are lost!
Thither my Lesbia's bird is flown,
And she is left his fate to moan;
Her tumid eyes with weeping sore;
For ah! her darling—is no more.

* Mellitus. † Pipiabat.

THE

THE

RETIRED SOLDIER.

Written near BATH, 1785.

Vera Effigies!

MATIUS, in action ſtrenuous, bold, and brave,
At home polite, in converſe gay or grave;
With knowledge to inſtruct, with wit to pleaſe,
Here ſpends his hours in health and ſtudious eaſe.
To form domeſtic happineſs complete,
The lovely partner of his bleſt retreat
Is prudent, kind, and gentle as the dove,
Alike the object of eſteem and love.

Thus

Thus liv'd in bliſs the firſt-form'd human pair;
He good and wiſe—ſhe tender, good, and fair.
With mutual love and nuptial fondneſs bleſt,
They, in each other, all the world poſſeſs'd.
Yet, 'midſt theſe joys, ſhould king or country call,
The ſoldier gladly would reſign them all;
The hermit march, let Britain ſpeak the word,
And quit his ſtaff to graſp the hero's ſword.

TO

THOMAS GAINSBOROUGH, Esq.

On his Portraits of the Three * Princesses.

SHALL Art with Nature, then, thus boldly vie,
Thus ape the glories of the Orient sky?
How dar'dst thou, mortal, impiously presume,
To imitate, with paint, celestial bloom?
How could'st thou on such radiant beauty gaze,
Uninjur'd by the splendor of its rays?
Some angel, sure, has lent his friendly aid,
To sketch the features of each royal maid.

* Princess Royal, Augusta, and Elizabeth.

What

What ſweetneſs ſoftens their majeſtic air!
What goodneſs beams from each diſtinguiſh'd
fair!
What ſpirit animates each lovely face!
And in each part what ſymmetry and grace!—
Such were the forms that bleſs'd the ſhepherd's
eyes
On Ida's mount, contending for the prize;
Such the three Graces of celeſtial mold,
That charm'd the ſculptors and the bards of
old.

Conſummate artiſt! ſay, from whence you
drew
The precepts of your art, ſo juſt, ſo true?
With freedom thus who bade thy pencil flow?
Such force, ſuch ſweetneſs in thy colours glow?
Haſt thou, to give perfection to thy piece,
Studied the works of ancient Rome or Greece?

Haſt thou ſurvey'd the celebrated * *rule*
Of ancient beauty? Or each modern ſchool
With critic eye compar'd, to ſtore thy mind
With all theſe wonders of a taſte refin'd?
Ah! no; thy matchleſs ſkill with ſcorn diſclaims
The fancied merit built on pompous names;
Like great Corregio, *Nature*'s pupil, fraught
With inborn genius, and by practice taught;
Who view'd e'en Raphael's works with conſcious pride,
And, "I'm a painter ſtill!" he nobly cried.
O'er ſeas or alps let other artiſts roam,
In queſt of beauties which you find at home;
Such charms our Britiſh nymphs alone can boaſt,
And he who paints them trueſt charms us moſt.

* The canon, or ſtandard of beauty, formed from a number of fine women, by Polycletus. PLIN. 34. 8.

1784.

O N

A YOUNG LADY,

SINGING TO HER HARPSICORD.

WHEN lovely Anna wakes th' harmonious ſtrings,
And in ſeraphic ſtrains the warbler ſings,
The rival of her mother's matchleſs tone,
(Whoſe ſkill each poliſh'd circle long has known)
The artleſs maid, unconſcious of her charms,
With thrilling raptures every boſom warms;
Each ſtring, that vibrates, ſpeeds the myſtic dart,
Whoſe ſympathetic force ſubdues the heart:

The

The liſtening throng th' electric influence
prove,
Catch ſudden flames, and kindle into love.
The young, the old, who, all attention, gaze,
The minſtrel's pow'r, by awful ſilence, praiſe.
Such rapturous ſcenes the bleſt above employ,
Where all is love, and harmony, and joy.

1784.

TO

A YOUNG LADY,

Diſtinguiſhed by her Genius for Painting, Muſic, and every other Accompliſhment.

WHEN genius thus, and ardent ſtudy, join'd,
With rich ideas ſtore the youthful mind;
And laudable ambition dares to ſoar
Where the bleſt few have wing'd their flight before;
When Reynolds checks the young enthuſiaſt's fire,
And Burney guides her hand to touch the lyre;

What lustre must adorn those pleasing arts,
From such instructors, and such brilliant parts!
A young * Angelica may feast our sight;
Our ears again † Cecilia may delight:
Music her ancient privilege may claim,
Of building towns, or savage beasts to tame;
And Painting view, on canvass or on paper,
New wonders from the pencil of Miss R—r.

* Angelica Kauffman.

† St. Cecilia.

TO

FLORELLA,

IN A VEIL.

"What means Luna in a Veil?"—REHEARSAL.

WITH cheeks more blooming than the vernal morn,
With all the charms that Beauty's Queen adorn,
With eyes more brilliant than the orient light,
Why will Florella *veil* them from our ſight?
Is it, that, conſcious of their dazzling blaze,
You wiſh to ſhield us from their ſcorching rays?
Alas! their utmoſt force we long to try,
Though, like bold Phaeton, we burn and die.

Laura, whoſe features wear the olive's hue,
Let her, and welcome, hide them from our view;
To pleaſe the ſight, when waning beauties fail,
They wiſely ſhun the world, and take the * *veil.*

* i. e. Retire to a Nunnery.

TO

MRS. L. S.

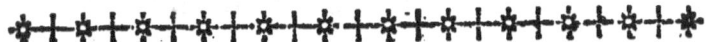

IN HER NURSERY.——4 June 1784.

WITH talents grac'd in public life to
ſhine!
With every charm that poets call divine!
When young Eliza, in the bloom of life,
Prefers the humble duties of a wife;
With tend'reſt air, amidſt her infant race,
Adds ſweet expreſſion to her lovely face;
Attentive to each dear, domeſtic call,
Slights the vain ſplendors of a birth-night ball;
How we deſpiſe the wretches that reſort

T' *endure* the painful vigils of a court ;
Who 'midſt the glittering, giddy circle roam,
In queſt of bliſs, which you enjoy at home !
Their charms (and charms perhaps they juſtly
boaſt)
Amidſt th' ambitious crowd eclips'd and loſt.
Yet one, e'en there, Eliza, may be ſeen,
Happy, like you—I need not name the Queen.

To ——— ———.

ADORN'D with every beauty, every grace,
A form celeſtial, and an angel's face;
With ſmiles that might a tyger's rage controul;
With eyes that dart ſweet tranſports to the ſoul:
Such is fair Lucia; yet, when I dare to praiſe
Her matchleſs beauties, or with rapture gaze,
She calls it *flattery*, ſays my love is blind,
And fancies charms, where ſhe no charms can find.

No, Lucia, no! 'tis you are blind, not I,
If *you* no charms, *I* no defects can ſpy.

Unconſcious of your merit, you diſclaim
Thoſe magic powers which every breaſt inflame;
But, what *your* modeſty conceals from you,
My throbbing heart convinces me is true,—
That you are more than painting can expreſs;
And, ſhould I *praiſe*, I cannot *love*, you leſs.

APOLOGY

For paſſing by a LADY in a Public Place.

THOUGH long I've worn love's pleaſing,
flowery chains,
And fix'd your image in my heart remains;
To which with rapture I, each riſing day,
Of vows and ſighs the ſacred incenſe pay;
Yet, when amidſt the crowd you bleſs'd my
ſight,
Your charms appear'd ſo raviſhingly bright,

With ſhame, with pride, my levity I own,
I *paſs'd you by*, as one I ne'er had known;
The image in my fancy pleas'd no more;
I did not *bow*, as I was wont before,
But I prepar'd an angel to *adore*.

1750.

To Mrs. —— —— ;

On ſome elegant Lines, inſcribed by her in my Gothic Cell.

AMIDST the hoary winter of my days,
To vanity long dead, and deaf to praiſe ;
With gloomy cares and ſecret griefs oppreſt,
Each ſpark of love expiring in my breaſt :
When thus I ſhare the kindneſs of a friend,
Whoſe cordial looks their ſocial influence lend ;
When Laura's wit, and more than manly ſenſe,
And female charms, a genial warmth diſpenſe ;
A gleam of joy lights up my evening hours,
No more the ſky with fancied tempeſts low'rs ;

I feel my heart with youthful ardour burn;
From ſixty to ſixteen at once return;
My Gothic Cell with W - - b-houſe may vie,
And grief and care my lonely ſhades defy.

To

To the Ducheſs of D——e,

On a recent Act of great Generoſity.

WHEN beauty ſhines untainted, 'midſt the rage
Of lawleſs pleaſure and a vicious age;
When Cavendish, tho' like an angel fair,
Yet more diſtinguiſh'd by a mother's care,
With each domeſtic virtue gilds the hours,
That peaceful glide 'midſt Chatſworth's bliſſful bowers;
Th' illuſtrious Dame the world's attention draws,
And e'en from vice extorts deſerv'd applauſe.

But, might the Muſe thoſe generous acts reveal,
Which liberal minds with anxious care conceal;
Tell, with what grief ſhe learns the tale of woe,
In what rich ſtreams ſhe bids her bounty flow;
What ſweet compaſſion melts her feeling heart,
Where every wretched object claims a part;
Impatient to relieve conceal'd diſtreſs,
The ſick to comfort, or the poor to bleſs:
Such deeds, more fit Heaven's favour to obtain,
Th' applauſe of earth-born reptiles muſt diſdain:
With faded luſtre Beauty's ſelf muſt ſhine;
Her charms are mortal, but kind acts divine!

To Mrs. ——.

BY love ſeduc'd, a young and thoughtleſs maid,
On marriage bent, a *father* diſobey'd;
The joys, but not the cares, of wedlock view'd,
And the fond dictates of her heart purſu'd:
Yet ſoon found cauſe her raſhneſs to repent;
For Heav'n, in wrath, a numerous offspring ſent;
And, as each day their daily wants grew more,
Each day diminiſh'd their too ſlender ſtore.
Their ſtate to mend, the ſtormy ſea they croſs'd;
Their lives were ſav'd—but all their ſubſtance loſt.

To

To you the culprits their diſtreſs impart;
You, too, obey the dictates of your heart;
And, tho' 'twas plain offended Heaven decreed
That poverty ſhould mark the *graceleſs* deed,
By ſtealth relieve them (bluſh at your offence!)
And thwart the vengeful plan of Providence.

22 Dec. 1785.

With a BATH TOY.

MOTTO, "*Think on me.*"

A TRIBUTE TO MERIT IN OBSCURITY.

BY age grown callous, though again my heart
From Myra's wit has felt love's pleaſing ſmart,
Let not my wiſhes too ambitious prove;
I aſk her *friendſhip* only—not her *love*.
To your connubial vows ſtill faithful be;
Yet deem it not a crime—to think on me.

NESTOR.

LEVITIES.

[illegible]

[illegible]

[illegible]

[illegible]

Somerset to wit. } To all Bards, Poets, or Poetaſters; Harpers, Pipers, and Fidlers; in Rhyme and Muſic, Dealers and Chapmen;

The COUNTY INFIRMARY

Sendeth Greeting;

Requeſting them to exert their ſkill, and reſtore that harmony, amongſt the Subſcribers, for finiſhing the Edifice, with which it ſo auſpiciouſly commenced.

I.

MUSIC has charms to calm the ſoul
With anxious cares oppreſt;
The human paſſions to controul,
Or tame a ſavage beaſt.

II. 'Tis

II.

'Tis her's to ſooth the pangs of love,
And pleaſing hopes impart;
The breaſt to ſoft compaſſion move,
To charity the heart.

III.

Ansty, in his enchanting verſe,
Could paint a ſcene of woe,
Which made * each churl unſtring his purſe,
And liberal ſums beſtow.

IV.

Amphion ſtruck his ſounding lyre,
The liſtening ſtones attend,
When lo! each tower and glittering ſpire
Of ſtately Thebes aſcend.

* This is no poetical fiction; a few elegant ſtanzas of that ingenious writer having raiſed ſome hundreds for the Hoſpital.

V.

Where winds the Thone * thro' fertile plains,
    A dome *began* to riſe,
A refuge for the ſickly ſwains—
    But now neglected lies.

VI.

A copious ſtream of bounty ran,
    This ſtructure to ſupply;
But, ere to build they well began,
    The ſource, alas! was dry.

VII.

Tune then your ſweet melodious lays,
    Ye votaries of Apollo!
And firſt a pile—of money raiſe!
    Our building ſoon will follow.

* Taunton.

VIII. Remove,

VIII.

Remove, at leaſt (for ſure you can)
This burthen from our ſhoulder;
Nor ſuffer ſuch a noble plan
In ruins thus to moulder:

IX.

Leſt travellers, that paſs this way,
Should turn it to a joke;
Should ſhake their heads, and *taunting* ſay,
Sure, *Taunton* men—are broke!

X.

If muſic then too feeble prove,
Or ſacred *pity*'s call,
Let *ſhame*, at leaſt, attention move;
Rouſe! neighbours, one and all!

XI. From

XI.

From diſſipation's ſcenes retreat,
  Ye thoughtleſs ſons of pleaſure!
Ye miſers! this good work complete,
  And hoard in heaven your treaſure.

Jan. 1786.

EPILOGUE TO THE FOUNDLING;

Acted by some private Gentlemen;

Spoken by Sir CHARLES RAYMOND.

HEY-day! how calm! how wondrous grave you sit!
Have we play'd ill? or does our play want wit?
A Comedy, I'm told, in days of yore,
Would set the pit—nay, boxes in a roar.
But comic humour's banish'd from the stage:
To laugh is vulgar, in this polish'd age;
Pathetic scenes, or sentiment's the *rage*.
And you have feeling—for I saw you weep.
I'm glad, at least, you did not fall asleep.

Yet

Yet poor Fidelia might excuſe your weeping,
For, faith! they almoſt forc'd her into keeping.
But Belmont's rakiſh plot at laſt miſcarried,
And my poor girl got tolerably married.
For virtue, ladies, is the *ſureſt* card;
And, firſt or laſt, will meet its full reward.
Well; but what think you of Roſetta's caſe?
'Egad, ſhe led her Colonel—*ſuch* a chace!—
Yet ſtrain'd full high the rigour of her charms;
And then at once came plump into his arms.
A few coquettiſh airs become the Fair;
But ah! dear ladies, take a *little* care:
Full many a nymph, that faſt and looſe has play'd,
And trifled with our hearts—has died a maid.
As for poor Faddle—that vile, ſenſeleſs calf,
He ſeems, indeed, *deſign'd* to make us laugh;
But when a virtuous lady's reputation
He ſtrives to blaſt—he moves our indignation.

In lower ſpheres tho' ſcoundrels may abound,
In *high* life are ſuch wretches to be found?
I hope friend More* was ſtill on fairy ground.

But could the gen'rous Belmont then employ
Such villains, his Fidelia to deſtroy?
That lovely maid, whoſe innocence to ſave,
His ſword had reſcued from a treach'rous knave.
See! then, the dire effects of lawleſs love!—
Yet, act like him, and from experience prove,
How much thoſe ſenſual flaſhes are o'er-paid
By the chaſte raptures of a virtuous maid;
And, to ſecure thoſe joys that laſt for life,
Diſcard the miſtreſs for a faithful wife!

* The author—and of many allegorical fables.

SOLILOQUY OF AN EPICURE.

—— *Epicuri de grege porcus.* HOR.

AL' IMPROVISO.

TO-DAY I with Palæmon dine;
Eat his Welch mutton—drink his wine;
With pine-apple, ice-cream, and jelly
Regale, and almoſt burſt my belly.
When full, with gratitude I burn,
To make my friend ſome ſlight return.
But lo! with mingled joy and ſorrow,
I ſee a roaſting-pig, to-morrow,
In damaſk napkin, clean and neat,
Truſs'd up, and ſent, juſt fit to eat;

And, what by me was more regarded,
With Latin distichs interlarded.
And thus, though pleas'd, I almost fret,
To find myself still more in debt;
For sure I feel no small vexation,
Thus overwhelm'd with obligation.

To feast on venison, hare, or pheasant,
Though some may think it vastly pleasant,
I would not value them a fig,
Compar'd with good Palæmon's pig.

Sweet, little, sharp-nos'd, harmless creature!
Though death has marr'd each sprightly feature,
Yet every tongue thy praise shall utter,
When, dress'd with currants, sage, and butter,
And spreading in a lordly dish,
You gratify each savoury wish!
Let purse-proud aldermen look big,
With scarlet gown and pompous wig,
Whilst we enjoy our dainty pig.

For

For ſure the Caledonian boar,
So fam'd, could not have pleas'd me more,
Nor eat ſo well, I'll hold a wager,
Though truſs'd by valiant Meleager.
Ye Gods! how nobly we ſhall dine!
Then fill the glaſs with—raiſin-wine,
And let each happy, little ſpark,
Drink, "All our friends at ——— Park;"
Nay, e'en my greyhound and fat ſpaniel,
Shall bleſs my Lady and Miſs D———l,
And little Will ſhall dance a jig,
In honour of our roaſting-pig.

DISTICHS.

From Martial.

WHILE round my cheeks the tedious tonſor goes,
Another beard beneath his razor grows.

On a Dramatic Poeteſs.

OLD Cowley in his tomb has long been laid,
But Mrs. Cowley *carries on the trade.*

On a Garden Seat, ill made.

ILL-FATED bench! in every ſenſe thou'rt wrong;
Though plain, not neat; though clumſy, yet not ſtrong.

Country-Houses.

SO fond are men of country-houses grown,
The town of Bath is all gone out of town.

THE

BACHELOR's CLUB.

To Sir Z———, Bart.

A Mind enlarg'd, with virtuous precepts
fraught,
The ſnares of vice, without experience, taught;
How can a youth of delicacy bear
The ſullied charms of a bought nymph to ſhare?
A wife, you ſay,'s expenſive;—true, my friend,
Yet ſure you'll find her cheapeſt, in the end:
And, when the days of dalliance are o'er,
A faithful ſpouſe is better than a wh–re.
Of this in high life you have proof full ample;
And e'en in humbler ſcenes, take one example:

A gallant

A gallant tradeſman, who, without a wife,
Taſted the pleaſures of a married life;
Yet liv'd by his aſſociates ſtill reſpected;
A *club* of jovial bachelors projected.
They met—talk'd politics—they drank—they ſmok'd—
And on connubial joys profanely jok'd.
But ſoon, alas! this hopeful ſcheme miſcarried,
For all the members died—or broke—or married.

TO

AN EXTEMPORE WRITER.

YOUR impromptu's (Lord Fanny ne'er wrote brighter)
All tend to prove, that you're a ready writer.
But when you give us things thus form'd in haſte,
You ſurely ſlight, or mock our want of taſte.
Your words muſt mean, in rational conſtruction,
That we're impatient for your choice production.

But,

But, Sir, we're not. Suppreſs your needleſs
fears;
Take time to poliſh—" Keep your piece nine
" years!"
Nay, not to bring you thus quite out o'breath,
We'd wait with patience, even till your death;
And, ſhould you loſe your manuſcript, or tear it,
With Chriſtian reſignation we muſt bear it.

TO

A DISAPPOINTED LOVER.

YOU wonder much, it ſeems, the maid you love
Should be a woman, and inconſtant prove;
And wonder more, that, in like piteous caſe,
I doggrel write, and wear a chearful face.
You lov'd in earneſt; *I* but lov'd for fun:
You'd hang or drown for love; *I* rhyme and pun.
The faithleſs nymph *you* load with angry curſes;
I vent my ſpleen in—lamentable verſes.

You

You hurt *yourſelf*, and not the worthleſs jilt;
I leave her to the ſtings of conſcious guilt.
  Say then, my friend, who acts the lover beſt?
You play the fool in earneſt; I in jeſt.

SUSANNA AND THE ELDERS;

Modernized from PRIOR.

TWO wicked elders once, we read,
With the ſame object ſmit, agreed
To force Suſanna to their arms,
And feaſt, by turns, upon her charms.
But ſhe, in conſcious virtue bold,
Began to bite, and ſcratch, and ſcold:
With cries and ſcreams th' affrighted maid
Brought all her footmen to her aid:
And thus preſerv'd her charms untainted;
And for her chaſtity was * ſainted.

* In the Popiſh calendar.

Yet,

Yet, haply, had the parties been
Juſt the reverſe of what we've ſeen;
Had ſhe been old, her lovers young,
Suſanna might have held her tongue;
Nay, grievouſly, perhaps, reſented
To 've had the raviſhers prevented.

"SWEET BATH!"

To a young LADY, on her departing Exclamation.

SWEET to the ſight, and ſweeter to the ſmell,
Sweet ſcene of joy, dear, lovely Bath, farewell!
Sweet are thy groves! but ſweeter far thy rooms;
Though Nature thoſe, and * Warren theſe perfumes.
Nor wonder Bath in aromatic ſmells,
And ſweeteſt odours, vulgar towns excels,

* A celebrated perfumer.

When

When P-rry, Kn-ght, and H-rton there diſpenſe
Each ſpicy drug that's grateful to the ſenſe:
At every turn you meet an eſſenc'd fop;
And all Arabia breathes from yonder ſhop:
There bounteous Heavens * their ſweeteſt blooms diſplay,
Sweet ſmiles, ſweet looks, and all the ſweets of May.
From Lyncomb Spa, to Bond or Ruſſel Street,
From Walcot to the Creſcent, all is ſweet—
Save when black clouds forebode impending rain,
And noiſome vapours riſe from every drain;
Then Liſbon's ſelf, or Edinburgh's fair ſtreet,
Ne'er fum'd the noſe with eſſences leſs *ſweet*:

* Some amiable young milliners of that name.

From

From Styx or Acheron, black ſtreams of hell,
Ne'er iſſu'd forth a more infernal ſmell;
Where ſinks and bogs thoſe various ſtenches join,
Sublime * by Burke, by Homer call'd *divine* †.

* See Sublime and Beautiful, Sect 33.

† Homer calls any ſtriking object *divine*.

THE

POCKET COMPANION;

OR,

LITTLE POLISH COUNT.

STANHOPE, in bulky tomes, attempts to teach
An art, which none from books could ever reach;
A syſtem of politeneſs—and the Graces,
Through all their winding paths, with labour traces.

TRUSLER, to teach young gentlemen good-breeding,
Without th' expence of ſuch *laborious* reading,
Wiſely

Wiſely diminiſhing his Lordſhip's plan,
Contracts th' enormous ſyſtem to a ſpan.
  But, if a living image you would ſee
Of true politeneſs in epitome—
See STANHOPE's precepts by example ſhewn,
And make the ſprightly Graces all your own—
The levee of the Poliſh Count attend,
And make the little gentleman your friend;
Or ſteal this miniature of man away,
And in your pocket wear him night and day.

TO THE

AUTHOR

OF

Some licentious Verſes on Miſs KN——.

WHOE'ER thou art, that ſhew'ſt thy want of ſenſe,
And not thy wit, at decency's expence;
I charge thee, rhymer, in Apollo's name,
Henceforth thy flaſhy Pegaſus to tame!
Nor dare to mount, where charms celeſtial ſhine,
Leſt the ſad fate of Phaeton be thine!

How

How dar'ſt thou thus Belinda's frown deſpiſe,
Or brave the vengeful lightning of her eyes?
Though mild as Flora, and by Nature kind,
She ſure muſt ſtrike ſuch bold ambition blind.
But when to vulgar eyes thy muſe unveils
Thoſe charms, which, chaſte as Dian, ſhe conceals;
With prying eyes thus wantonly invade
The ſnowy boſom of the lovely maid;
Acteon's fate expect, thou ſaucy clown!
Converted to a brute, and hunted down!
But, bolder yet, on rhyming wildly bent,
Thou rudely dar'ſt thy amorous wiſhes vent;
Some low-born proſtitute thy fancy warms,
Who, wont to ſell her mercenary charms,
Might gladly bleſs her Grub-ſtreet poet's arms.

May'ſt thou then take the lewd * Ixion's place,
And for Heaven's Queen ſome dirty cloud em-
brace.

20 Dec. 1784.

* Who attempting the chaſtity of Juno, had a cloud ſlipt into his arms.

THE

QUAKER'S ADVICE

TO THE

* MAN IN BLACK CLOTHING.

WHAT ſpirit mov'd thee, Man in Black,
Thus neighbour A—ſty to attack?
I tell thee, friend, thou'ſt caught a tartar;
If thou art ſmart, thy foe is ſmarter.
What tempted thee to thruſt thy noſe
Where thou'dſt no *call* to interpoſe?
Let the ungodly rhyme and joke;
Why ſhould their mirth thy wrath provoke?

* This alludes to an unprovoked attack on a worthy character, ſome time ſince.

Though

Though not invited to Batheaston,
Thou hast more spiritual joys to feast on;
Thy business is with Holy Bible:.
Deal not in vain and carnal libel.

As well might'st thou, when drest in black,
'Gainst whited wall have rubb'd thy back;
Or had a barber run against ye,
As thus provoke the man call'd A—y.

Though loth to give e'en culprits pain,
"He beareth not the quill in vain."
And if, my friend, thy deeds are evil,
Thou'lt find this lamb a very D-vil.
Henceforth the ways of wit renounce,
Taught to be wise by Humphry Pounce.

LAMENTATIONS.

WERTER to CHARLOTTE.

(A little before his Death.)

O Charlotte! Charlotte! all-accompliſh'd maid,
To whom my heart its homage long has paid;
In whom is center'd all that's good or fair;
Whoſe ſmiles attractive, whoſe enchanting air,
To every heart their influence extend,
And make a *lover*, where you meant a friend:
Whoſe ruby lips and melting voice diſpenſe
Melliſluous ſounds, with more than manly ſenſe;
Whoſe waving locks and ivory neck impart
The faireſt model for the ſculptor's art:

WERTER TO CHARLOTTE,

(A little before his Death.)

O Charlotte! Charlotte! all-accomplish'd
maid,
To whom my heart its homage long has paid;
In whom is center'd all that's good or fair;
Whose smiles attractive, whose enchanting air,
To every heart their influence extend,
And make a *lover*, where you meant a friend:
Whose ruby lips and melting voice dispense
Mellifluous sounds, with more than manly sense;
Whose waving locks and ivory neck impart
The fairest model for the sculptor's art:

O lovely Charlotte! how ſhall I controul
The thrilling raptures that poſſeſs my ſoul?
How bid my paſſion yield to Reaſon's voice,
When Reaſon's ſelf muſt juſtify my choice?
Yet, tho' thy charms, the ſource of every joy,
My thoughts by day, my dreams by night employ;
Tho' thy lov'd image, by gay fancy dreſt,
With more than youthful ardor fires my breaſt;
Woe to the man that would thy heart beguile,
And that angelic ſoul with guilt defile!
Who'd dare to violate the nuptial rights,
(That ſacred bond which one to one unites).
I *love*, but *covet* not, good Albert's wife,
Nor would deſtroy, my friend, thy peace for life.
But when at length thoſe bliſsful realms we gain,
Where no connubial claims our thoughts reſtrain;

Where

Where ſelfiſh, human laws ſhall ceaſe to bind,
And univerſal love reigns unconfin'd;
Then, free as air, congenial ſouls ſhall meet,
And ſex, with holy rapture, ſex ſhall greet:
Then will I ſnatch dear Charlotte to my arms,
And chaſtly revel in celeſtial charms:
Ecſtatic bliſs ſhall groſſer love ſucceed,
And Charlotte make that ſcene—a heav'n in-
deed.

SUICIDE.

RASH youth, forbear! O lay that poniard by;
Nor boldly thus the wrath of Heaven defy!
Contend not with thy God, in impious strife,
But calmly bear th' allotted ills of life;
Nor from thy station treach'rously withdraw,
Assign'd by Heaven's inviolable *law*.
"With grief, with pain, or poverty opprest,
"No ray of hope to cheer the tortur'd breast;
"Or

" Or with ill-fortune, ſay, the wretch has ſtrove,
" Neglect of friends, or pangs of ſlighted love;
" What *law* commands *ſuch* wretches to endure
" Thoſe deſperate evils, which admit no cure?"
—The firſt primæval law, by Heav'n impreſt,
At man's creation, on the human breaſt,
The love of life—which nothing can controul,
Till loſs of reaſon ſtupifies the ſoul.
Self-preſervation is God's firm decree;
Can *ſelf-deſtruction* then from guilt be free?
The fear of death the ſtouteſt heart appalls,
Then liſten to her voice—'tis Nature calls.
Haſt thou no offspring, no dear, faithful wife,
By love, by intereſt, anxious for thy life?
No aged father, or more tender mother?
No friend more dear than ſiſter or than brother?

If thou thyself canst mock the poniard's smart,
Ah! plunge not thus the dagger in *their* heart!

But say then, whence these miseries arise?
Though men are foolish, God is good and wise;
By whose kind plan, 'tis evident, mankind
Were for a life of happiness design'd.
Thy griefs then spring from luxury and vice;
Thy poverty, perhaps, from cards and dice.
Does love, like Werter's, thy fond breast inspire?
Let reason quench, at once, th' adult'rous fire:
Nor think t' intrude amidst the blest above,
A soul defil'd with sin and guilty love.

As death to *murder* is by Heaven decreed,
Self-murder surely is a fouler deed,
And death eternal must that crime succeed;
For Mercy's self, though eager to relent,
Expects, at least, our crimes we should repent;

But

But what atonement can the wretch devise,
Who wilfully affronts his God—and dies?
  Then yield not, coward-like, to transient woe,
But bravely, like a Christian, face thy foe;
Dare to be wretched, if thou dar'st to sin,
Lest, when these pains thou'st ended, *worse* begin.

ON

Miſs MARIA LINLEY,

Singing an Hymn as ſhe expired.

I.

WHEN languid now her fluttering breath
Maria faintly drew;
She ſaw, beyond the ſhades of death,
Heaven opening to her view.

II.

Regardleſs of her dying pains,
Her voice ſhe ſtrove to raiſe;
Rejoicing in ſeraphic ſtrains
To chant her Maker's praiſe.

III. Her

III.

Her ſoul, in virgin luſtre bright,
Burſt through the mortal clay,
And, ſoaring to the realms of light,
Exulting wing'd its way.

IV.

Thus from her neſt, with towering wings,
We view the ſweet lark riſe;
With joy her matin notes ſhe ſings,
And warbling mounts the ſkies.

ON THE

ESSAYS AND POEMS

Of a LADY lately deceaſed.

WILT thou theſe little volumes then
perуſe?
Hope not to wanton with ſome ſportive Muſe,
Or with ſome ſprightly Noveliſt to rove,
Amidſt the flowery labyrinths of love.
No; think ſome holy Veſtal tunes the lyre,
In ſolemn ſtrains true wiſdom to inſpire;
Or ſacred Oracles ſage truths impart,
To calm the paſſions, and to mend the heart.

From

From ſome ſtrange cauſe, which med'cine ne'er could reach,
JANETTA loſt her faculty of ſpeech;
Hard fate! though bleſt with ſenſe, tho' fair and young,
A nymph debarr'd her privilege of tongue!—
Yet, young JANETTA ſate, when paſt relief,
"Like patience on a tomb, and ſmil'd at grief*."
Happy, amidſt the circle of her friends,
Their converſe ſweet, in ſilence, ſhe attends;
She works, reads, writes, but all, alas! in vain,
Amuſement *ſooth'd*, but could not eaſe her pain:
Loſt to the world, by various ills oppreſt,
At length the meek, mute ſufferer ſunk to reſt.

* Shakeſpeare.

In

In years tho' young, in wisdom's school mature,
Who learn'd *such* ills with patience to endure.
But lo! her death a miracle succeeds,
Beyond the saints of legendary creeds;
" Though dead, she speaks" such truths as saint or sage
Has rarely spoke, in any clime or age.
Check'd by her virgin diffidence no more,
Her weeping friends unlock her secret store:
No gold or toys her cabinet display'd;
No tribute to her charms by lovers paid.
With pious maxims, deep reflections fraught,
Pour'd from a heart, by sad experience taught
To pity human woes; and warm to raise,
The grateful hymn to her Creator's praise.
Pleas'd with her prose, enchanted with her song,
We scarce regret the silence of her tongue;

A ma-

A malady, whoſe aid, in mercy given,
A ſaint on earth, an angel form'd for heaven.
As Milton painted Nature's charms, though blind,
Though mute, JANETTA ſhall inſtruct mankind.

TO

Dr. JOHNSON,

On his intended Tour to the Continent.

IN youth a glorious * *Rambler*, why this rage
For *rambling* now, my friend, worn down with age?
Why blame the Sovereign †, who, both good and wise,
The *means* of *rambling* to thy wish denies?
G——e lets his fools thro' Europe idly roam,
But keeps his wise and learned men at home.

* His celebrated papers, so called.

† Who refused to increase his pension for that purpose.

ON

ON THE

DEATH of the late Dr. WILSON.

Sequiturque patrem propè passibus æquis.

THE good man hopes to leave a virtuous race,
But the good root the branches oft disgrace:
A worthy sire, a worthless heir succeeds,
And in the child the parent's bosom bleeds.
E'en Tully's son, tho' bred in wisdom's school,
Became ('tis said) a sot—if not a fool.
But lo! with joy the pious * WILSON view'd
His own fair image in his son renew'd;

* The good Bishop of Sodor and Man.

The

The Prelate ſhone—with ſolar luſtre bright;
The Son appear'd with more than borrow'd
light.
Alike their public ſpirit, unconfin'd,
Their charity—was love of human-kind.
Wherever modeſt merit * liv'd oppreſs'd,
Or virtue pin'd by poverty diſtreſs'd,
His active ſpirit ſought it and reliev'd;
And then alone, like noble Titus, griev'd,
When vice (which ne'er true intereſt under-
ſtood)
Depriv'd him of the bliſs of doing good.
But now that liberal hand is ſtretch'd no more,
To aid th' afflicted, or relieve the poor.

* The world is obliged to Dr. Wilſon, for encouraging Leland to write his excellent View of the Deiſtical Writers. See Preface.

Mature

Mature in years, with friends and fortune
blefs'd,
The venerable patriarch funk to reft.
For him the orphan drops the filial tear,
For him the prifoner mourns with grief fincere;
Who ne'er unmov'd could hear diftrefs com-
plain,
Or let a fellow-creature plead in vain.
Yet thefe are tranfient bleffings, tho' fo great;—
To make his deeds of charity complete,
In humble hope the thoughtlefs foul to fave,
His father's pious Works he nobly gave,
In lafting types, to iffue from the prefs—
Whofe faving truths pofterity fhall blefs.
The Prelate's Works fhall ftill extend his fame;
And the good Son adorn the Father's name.

ELEGY

E L E G Y

ON THE

DEATH of Dr. SAMUEL JOHNSON.

To Sir Joshua Reynolds.

MATURE in age, with fame, with honour crown'd,
For virtue reverenc'd, as for wit renown'd;
Whose bosom glow'd with purest precepts fraught;
Whose life express'd each precept which he taught.
Such Johnson was—but is, alas! no more!
Let Literature herself the loss deplore;

With Piety and Virtue by her ſide,
In ſable mourn their guardian and their pride.

Though life is frail, all human glories vain,
Yet Johnſon's bays unfaded ſhall remain;
His works ſurvive, to future ages dear,
And lateſt times *his* memory revere;
Who firſt * from faſhion's laws our language freed
(A taſk, where none but Johnſon could ſucceed;)
With genius, taſte, and erudition join'd,
Each term abſtruſe, each dubious phraſe defin'd,
And fix'd the ſtandard of that wavering tongue,
In which himſelf had written—Pope had ſung.

As plann'd by him, e'en dictionaries pleaſe;
He moral truths has taught with claſſic eaſe:
Add, that his writings blend, thro' every page,
The chriſtian hero, and the learned ſage.

* His Dictionary.

Our Poets' * works with critic ſkill he weigh'd,
Their faults, their beauties, and their lives diſ-
play'd.
From him, to judge with freedom we may learn,
And ſolid ſenſe from empty ſound diſcern.
Himſelf correct, he hardly knew to ſpare
Thoſe bards, who boldly vend unfiniſh'd ware.
Unaw'd by names, if by too rigid laws
Some † bards he judg'd, who merit juſt applauſe,
With equal candour, by a gentler teſt,
He others tried, whom rival wits oppreſs'd.

* His Lives of our Poets.

† A new æra or ſchool of poetry ſeems to have commenced with Mr. Gray, as different from the ſimplicity of Addiſon, Pope, and Parnel, as Pindar's or Horace's Odes from Homer or Virgil; and, as the *ſublime*, which is the characteriſtic of Gray, often borders on *obſcurity*, ſome paſſages in his poems might, perhaps, be interpreted according to the *inclination* of the reader.

E'en

E'en Watts and Blackmore, whoſe flat ſtrains abound
With pious traits, in him a patron found.
But while we juſtly praiſe what Johnſon wrote,
Are then his humble charities forgot?
Himſelf not rich, he ſhar'd his ſlender ſtore
With thoſe who *were*, but ought not to *be*, poor;
Sought modeſt merit, in its dark abode,
The naked cloth'd, and gave the hungry food.
Nor were his friendſhips leſs his joy or pride,
With whom in friendſhip Garrick liv'd and died
And Reynolds, doom'd, alas! his friend to mourn,
And deck with cypreſs wreaths his hallow'd urn;
Whoſe matchleſs ſkill has done, what painting can,
That thoſe who read his works, may *view* the man.

Nor, Thurlow, thou diſdain thy meed of praiſe,
Whoſe bounty ſtrove thy drooping friend to raiſe,
If haply warmer climes might yet reſtore
That health, which medicine could aſſiſt no more.

Stern foe to vice, by virtue's friends careſs'd,
Thus Johnſon liv'd, with learned leiſure bleſt;
Happy through life, yet happier in his end,
Who, dying, claim'd his Saviour for his friend*.

Ob. 13 Dec. 1784.

* Though Dr. Johnſon, by the officious kindneſs of ſome of his friends, may be ſomewhat lowered in the opinion of the public; yet the author of *The Rambler*, and of that great work, *The Engliſh Dictionary*, will always merit the ſlight encomiums here paſſed upon him.

It has been obſerved, that no man is an hero, in the ſight of his valet de chambre; and no author can appear *great*, if ſhewn to the world in the diſhabille of his thoughts, and in the moſt trifling domeſtic employments.

EPILOGUE.

EPILOGUE.

MY book, you tell me, "little more
"contains
"Than fulſome praiſe and panegyric ſtrains;
"Or haply, here and there, an harmleſs meſs
"Of ridicule on fops and female dreſs."
Merit, I own, my muſe delights to praiſe;
But, though they're dull, think not they're venal lays,
Which beauty's or which virtue's charms inſpire:
'Tis truth, 'tis gratitude, that tunes my lyre.
Each generous act with pleaſure I commend;
Who makes a good man happy—is *my* friend:

The

The nymph that with her beauty feaſts my
ſight,
Beſtows a boon—of innocent delight.
To works of Art my muſe a tribute pays,
And Nature's charms with rapture ſhe ſurveys.
But if, perchance, I cenſure fop or fool,
'Tis Folly, not the Man, I ridicule.
Howe'er my ſcorn or cenſure be expreſs'd,
Nor pride nor malice harbour in my breaſt.
To vice or folly though I am not blind;
I love, and I wiſh well—to all mankind:
Their good and *my* amuſement is my view——
But you're aſleep—Adieu! my friend, adieu!

FINIS.

www.ingramcontent.com/pod-product-compliance
Lightning Source LLC
Chambersburg PA
CBHW020112030726
47498CB00006B/2075
9783744689410